"Warm, funny and devastatingly honest. An incredibly insightful story full of hope and resilience."
—**Dr Amir Khan**, *Sunday Times* Bestselling Author and Resident Doctor for ITV's *Lorraine* and *Good Morning Britain*

"The commonly held view that the widespread stigma attached to mental illness is the result of misinformation in the population has spawned a wave of well-meaning, but largely ineffective, public-education campaigns. The fact is that stigma is largely the result of the reality of the lived experience of persons with mental illness, characterised by exclusion and violence, not least in the health care system. The battle against stigma must begin with placing the lives of humans at the heart of all conversations about mental illness and this book is an exemplar of such an endeavour. Professor Hankir offers an inspiring rebuke to the nihilism that prevails in society about mental illness through the courage, resilience and hope of his personal journey."
—**Vikram Patel**, Paul Farmer Professor and Chair of Global Health and Social Medicine, Harvard Medical School, USA

"Professor Hankir's incredible story describing his extraordinary experiences is an important contribution to the mental health literature. Essential reading especially

for persons living with a mental health condition, their loved ones and carers and mental health practitioners."
—**Professor Tamsin Ford,** Head of the Department of Psychiatry, University of Cambridge

"An honest, engaging and most of all, hopeful book."
—**Adam Kay,** BAFTA-Winning, Multi-Million-Bestselling Author, TV Writer and Performer

"A story of an extraordinary, challenged and packed life in which Ahmed bravely recounts, with every humility and grace, the life journey that has made him a unique and powerful role model for all who face adversity in their lives. This book is a toolkit for turning hopelessness into success, sadness into deep joy and stigmatisation into fuel for positively transforming others' lives. Please, please, please read Professor Hankir's inspirational book, it will change your life."
—**Professor Ged Byrne MBE,** Director Global Health, Consultant Surgeon, NHS England

"Embracing a world of life challenges, and guided by his expertise, both personal and professional, Professor Ahmed Hankir has given us a gift—a true breakthrough. This timely book reminds us that mental health "flaws" can be tools: that vulnerability and shared humanity can be deployed to heal our fellow wounded travellers."
—**Professor Andrés Martin,** Riva Ariella Ritvo Professor, Yale Child Study Center and Medical Director, Children's Psychiatric Inpatient Service at Yale-New Haven Children's Hospital, Connecticut USA. Editor Emeritus, *Journal of the American Academy of Child and Adolescent Psychiatry*

Breakthrough

A Story of Hope, Resilience and Mental Health Recovery

Dr Ahmed Hankir

CAPSTONE
A Wiley Brand

This edition first published 2024
© 2024 Ahmed Hankir

Registered Office(s)
John Wiley & Sons, Inc., 111 River Street, Hoboken, NJ 07030, USA
John Wiley & Sons Ltd, The Atrium, Southern Gate, Chichester, West Sussex, PO19 8SQ, UK

For details of our global editorial offices, customer services, and more information about Wiley products visit us at www.wiley.com.

Wiley also publishes its books in a variety of electronic formats and by print-on-demand. Some content that appears in standard print versions of this book may not be available in other formats.

Library of Congress Cataloging-in-Publication Data is Available:

ISBN 9780857089724 (Paperback)
ISBN 9780857089687 (ePDF)
ISBN 9780857089670 (ePub)

Cover Design: Wiley
Cover Images: © kichigin19/Adobe Stock; © lamyai/Adobe Stock

SKY10072521_041124

Do not go gentle into that good night. . . Rage, rage against the dying of the light. . .

Dylan Thomas

If living with a mental health condition has taught me anything, it's that the cognitive capacity of the mind to receive and to conceive ideas is something that should never, ever be taken for granted.

There have been periods in my life during which my mind was so shattered that it was unable to comprehend and concentrate and to produce any meaningful or coherent thoughts. Reading a book let alone writing one would have been an impossible task during those trying times.

I am immeasurably grateful and extremely fortunate that I was able to recover and regain my cognitive powers. That being said, recovery, certainly for me, was a gradual, slow and painful process that took many years.

I, however, was one of the lucky ones. Far too many of us tragically continue to experience severe symptoms of a mental health condition, no matter what we do or how hard we try.

I think of people living with bipolar affective disorder, schizophrenia and schizoaffective disorder. Those held captive by paranoid and persecutory delusions or tormented by terrifying voices and visions. Persons at the behest of sudden and extreme fluctuations in mood, which can be hugely distressing to the degree that they are associated with the highest suicide rates.

Many of us perhaps take for granted the stability of our moods and/or are unaware of how immobilising and disabling psychotic symptoms (delusions and hallucinations) can be.

I also think of those with dementia and other types of neurodegenerative conditions who are unable to express themselves due to the devastating fragmentation of memory.

My heart breaks for persons living with eating disorders, which have the highest mortality rate of all psychiatric disorders. It weeps for those amongst us living with anxiety disorders such as obsessive compulsive disorder and post-traumatic stress disorder the intrusive symptoms of which can be enormously crippling and debilitating.

Not enough is being done for people living with these cruel conditions. Not enough awareness is being raised. Not enough specialist support – social care and mental healthcare – is available. The quality of that care, when it is available, has also often been described as poor and inadequate.

The human rights violations of persons living with severe mental health conditions and psychosocial disabilities and the stigma and discrimination they face is also another major issue and is a stain on our collective conscience.

The catalogue of injustices goes on and on. A government is judged based on how they treat the most vulnerable in society. If we look at how people living with severe mental illnesses are being treated, the Government has failed spectacularly.

This is unacceptable. We need to do more. We must do more. People living with severe mental health conditions have been let down for far too long and deserve better.

More attention must be given. More resources must be allocated. More high-quality and easy-to-access specialist support must be provided.

I dedicate this book to persons who cannot formulate and express their thoughts because of the severity of their symptoms and how injured their minds are. But also, to those amongst us who are able to speak out but who are stigmatised and shunned and towards whom a deaf ear is turned. This book is dedicated to the voiceless individuals who haven't been given a platform to amplify their views and share their stories and testimonies but instead are ridiculed and silenced.

Our hearts grieve for you and go out to you and to your loved ones and to all those who provide you with informal support. You are the true unsung mental health heroes, and you deserve so much more than a dedication.

I hope this book raises awareness of your plight.

But also, of your dignity and grace as you continue to fight that good fight,

And as you 'rage, rage against the dying of the light . . .'.

Dr Ahmed Hankir

Ontario

Canada October 2023

Contents

Contents

About the Author

Dr Hankir, MBChB, MRCPsych, is Consultant Psychiatrist (Canada and UK), Honorary Visiting Professor at the School of Medicine, Cardiff University (UK), Assistant Professor of Psychiatry at Western University (Canada), Professor of Academic Psychiatry at Carrick Institute for Graduate Studies (USA), Senior Research Fellow at the Centre for Mental Health Research in association with Cambridge University (UK) and Public Engagement and Education Lead at the World Health Organization Collaborating Centre for Mental Health and Human Rights, Institute of Mental Health, Nottingham University (UK).

Dr Hankir's research interests include global and Muslim mental health and pioneering and evaluating innovative interventions that reduce mental health-related stigma and Islamophobia and he has published widely in these areas. Dr Hankir has co-edited three textbooks on psychiatry and religion with Senior Members of the American Psychiatric Association. He is a public speaker and lecturer and has been invited to deliver talks at some of the most prestigious universities in the world including Harvard, Stanford, Yale, McGill, Toronto, Cambridge,

Oxford, London, Padua and Coimbra. Dr Hankir has been consulted by the World Health Organization (WHO) for his expertise on mental health and human rights and has also been consulted by the New Zealand Government for advice on the psychological consequences of the Christchurch Mosque terror attacks. He is the recipient of multiple prestigious awards most notably the 2022 WHO Director General Award for Global Health.

Dr Hankir identifies as a survivor and is passionate about empowering, dignifying and humanising persons living with mental health conditions. Dr Hankir is also passionate about broadening access into medical school for persons from low-income backgrounds. He enjoys going for long walks in parks, immersing himself in nature, travelling and drinking coffee in local cafes. He also enjoys cycling, running and raising funds for charities.

Preface

In July 2005, I was 22 years old. I woke up one morning in a dilapidated and squalid terrace house in Moss Side, the roughest area in Manchester, England and I suddenly started to cry irrepressibly and inconsolably. For months I had been in denial that I was mentally unwell despite 'the conflagration in my wake'; whilst the bridges in Lebanon were burning literally (this was during the 2006 Lebanon–Israel War, which was a factor that contributed to my 'breaking point'), I had burnt bridges in the metaphorical sense with my very own family and people who, at the time, I considered to be my closest friends. I had been forced to interrupt medical school and I was impoverished, shunned and ostracised. The 'insight switch' abruptly turned on and I was completely overwhelmed with reality. What had I done? What had happened? All of my hard work to get into medical school flushed down the drain in what seemed like the blink of an eye. So, I cried, and I cried, and I continued to cry until there were no more tears left for me to shed. It was the loneliest, most isolated, and afraid I have ever felt in my entire life. If ever there was a rock bottom, this was it. Later that night, I would leave the house and walk up and down Oxford Road.

The prospectus that was posted to me before I started medical school in 2003 stated that this was one of the busiest bus routes in Europe. I would look towards the oncoming traffic and thoughts of thrusting myself under one of the buses flooded my mind. 'This pain is just too unbearable. . .' I would think to myself. . .

=====

May 2022:

You know that feeling when you are waiting for the President of France to finish giving his speech so that you can give yours?! World leaders and health ministers from all 194 member states of the World Health Organization (WHO) had gathered for the WHO World Health Assembly at the Palace of Nations – the headquarters for WHO – in Geneva. And there he was, the charismatic Emmanuel Macron himself, exuding panache and mesmerising the audience, me included, with his manner.

Every year, the Director General of the WHO the honourable Dr Tedros Adhanom Ghebreyesus selects individuals and groups to receive the WHO Director General Award for Global Health. In 2022, I was selected to be a recipient of the award. Words cannot begin to describe how I was feeling. I vividly remember when Dr Tedros invited me onto the world stage. I'll never forget the moment when he made eye contact with me and welcomed me with warmth, compassion, kindness and sincerity. My life flashed before my eyes as I was approaching him. All the challenges, setbacks, suffering, struggling, traumas, difficulties, discrimination, poverty, stigmatisation. All of it came flooding back. Despite my best efforts, I was unable to hold back the tears. But Dr Tedros comforted and consoled me. He fathomed the enormity of this occasion for me and I felt safe, secure and strong in his presence. We embraced each other in front of our audience and in front of the world. Following a brief exchange of words with the Director General, I felt empowered, inspired and dignified to launch into my acceptance speech. Of all the speeches that were delivered during the 2022 WHO World Health Assembly High Level Welcome, mine was the only one to have received a standing ovation. After giving my speech, I was overwhelmed with emotion again however only this time, I was not shedding tears of sorrow. These were tears of joy. This was the proudest moment in my life. . . .

Introduction and Mission Statement

This book will trace my recovery journey from the man I was in 2005, that is, a 'hopeless, impoverished, shunned and suicidal service user from a Black, Asian, and Minority Ethnic (BAME) background with mental illness' to the man I am today: 'an empowered survivor, mental health advocate, professor and consultant psychiatrist'. There are multiple versions of ourselves residing within us. These two versions of myself are not necessarily dichotomous or mutually exclusive; you can be a consultant psychiatrist living with a mental health condition and that, of course, is nothing to be ashamed about.

I identify as a Wounded Healer and this book approaches mental health from the dual perspectives of psychiatrist or 'mental healthcare provider' and psychiatric patient or 'mental healthcare receiver'. Whilst there are many books about mental health from 'Experts by Personal Experience', for example, survivors, 'service users', patients, and many books from 'Experts by Professional Experience' (psychiatrists, professors) there are not so many books from 'Experts by Personal and Professional Experience'(EPPEs). I was not able to find a single memoir/autobiographical narrative from a psychiatrist who recovered from a mental health condition who is from a BAME background (i.e., a 'BAME EPPE') despite the fact that people from BAME backgrounds are over-represented in mental healthcare services and that a substantial proportion of the psychiatric workforce in the UK (over 40%) are International Medical Graduates (IMGs) who are from BAME backgrounds. Racism is a huge problem in society and psychiatry and has been catapulted deeper into public consciousness since the murder of George Floyd in the United States and the #blacklivesmatter movement. The Royal College of Psychiatrists has appointed Presidential Leads in Racial Equality to address racism in psychiatry (both patients and psychiatrists report being victims of racism) and the American Psychiatric Association, 'Apologised to Black, Indigenous, and People of Colour for its support of structural racism in psychiatry. . . .'

This book also contains short stories about the people who have mental health difficulties who I have been fortunate to assess and provide care to whilst working in the frontline of the National Health Service (NHS), UK during the pandemic.

This book is aimed at people living with mental health problems, their family members, friends and caregivers. It is also targeted at health and social care workers and the general public. In other words, this book is for everyone because mental health is everyone's business and it concerns us all. The most important group, however, are people who themselves are living with mental health difficulties. It is my hope that you will be able to draw upon this book for guidance, solace and advice and that you can learn lessons from the many 'mistakes' that I have made. Perhaps you will be able to identify with me and relate to my experiences – both the symptoms and the stigma associated with mental health conditions. This identification can be validating and make you feel less alone and less ashamed. I hope that by sharing my story, it will give you hope that people living with mental health conditions can, with the right support and resources, recover, function again and realise their potential, even their dreams. . . .

Mission Statement

The mission statement of this book was informed by the many, many people I have been fortunate to meet (in person or online) over the years whilst the seed of this book was in germination. It is therefore not 'my' mission statement but rather 'our' mission statement:

- Dignify, empower and humanise people living with mental health conditions. . .
- Disseminate the message that 'there is no shame in experiencing mental health difficulties. . . '
- Instil hope into the hearts, minds, bodies, and souls of people living with a mental health condition that recovery is a reality for the many and not the few. . .

- Let people with mental health difficulties know that 'they are not alone. . .' and that 'they should not suffer in silence. . .'
- Provide people with a resource and the tools for mental health recovery, resilience and redemption. . .
- Offer an insight into the heart, mind, body and soul of a man from a Black, Asian and Minority Ethnic Background who has recovered from a mental health condition and who has, dare I say it, done rather well for himself (not despite his condition but because of it. . .). In other words, a person living with a mental health condition who has not only survived, but thrived. . .
- Demonstrate the colossal power that the performing arts and storytelling has in mental healthcare and education. . .

I

Seeking Sanctuary

Why am I as I am? To understand that of any person, his whole life, from birth must be reviewed. All of our experiences fuse into our personality. Everything that ever happened to us is an ingredient.

Malcolm X

Malcolm's words ring true with me although I do have a point of contention with them. I would argue that events that occur even before our birth can strongly influence who we eventually become and our vulnerability to (and our resilience against) developing mental health conditions. I am also sure that the epigeneticists amongst us would say that influences that occur in-utero also play an important role.

To illustrate the above point, I will briefly trace my father's journey. Dr Zakaria Hankir was one of 13 children. It was not unusual in that time and place to have large families. Dad was born in the ancient Phoenician city of Sidon in south Lebanon, the first child amongst his siblings not to be born in Haifa, a coastal city in a territory that was named Palestine during my grandparents' generation (and in the hearts and minds of many will forever be named as such). My grandfather Ahmed Hankir (after whom I was named) worked in Haifa for many years. My father said that my grandfather's accent was strongly Palestinian, so much so that my father acquired the Palestinian accent from his father even though my father himself never lived in Palestine. Later, when my father moved back to Lebanon his accent would influence which patients would consult him, such was and remains the sectarian divide in Lebanon.

My paternal grandfather was marred by tragedy when he was rendered an orphan at a young age. He did not receive a formal education and had limited literary ability; however, he was renowned for his physical strength. My grandfather migrated to Haifa due to its economic prosperity. Whilst there, he sold ful and hummus to the local townspeople as he would walk up and down the sun scorched and unmarked streets of Haifa with his trusted business partner, his donkey! In 1948, my grandfather was forced to flee Haifa with hundreds of thousands of Palestinians during what is known as 'the Nakba' or 'the catastrophe' after the state of Israel declared sovereignty (there is so much more that can be said and that has been said about 'the Nakba', however, that is beyond the scope of this book. What I will say is that 'the Nakba' continues to have a profound impact on all those who were affected, none more so than the people of Palestine who were forcibly displaced and dispossessed. 'The catastrophe' is a scar that remains indelibly etched on the collective consciousness of the people of Palestine and continues to be a source of unresolved trauma). Leaving all his belongings behind, Grandad returned to his native city of Sidon setting up a ful and hummus shop over there. My grandfather had an extraordinary work ethic and the highest of standards. Word of the high quality of his food and how delicious the meals were spread throughout the city and indeed all the way to the capital, Beirut. Former Prime Ministers of Lebanon Rafic Hariri and Fouad Siniora would frequent my grandfather's establishment when they were children. It was and remains a source of great family pride. I never got to meet my Grandad, may he rest in peace, the man whose name I bear. He passed away before I was born. From time to time my gaze turns skyward where I pray his soul will ascend. I imagine him looking down on me, proud of his grandson, Dr Ahmed Hankir. It makes me emotional just thinking about it.

Although not as opulent as Haifa, Sidon was not without its charm and allure. Our teachers in Lebanon would harken to centuries gone by and proudly and patriotically say to us that the port in Sidon enabled the city to flourish and consequently the region at the time was a commercial hub. My memories of Sidon are of the crusader castle that can be seen whenever one passes by the coastline of the Old City. It is all the more stunning at night time when the lights would be turned on. I still have an affinity towards Sidon. The place and its people have shaped my character and values so profoundly. It was where I spent my formative years after all and it was just prior to the devastating fragmentation of my family. I will elaborate on the impact that living in Sidon had on my identity later in this book.

My father was from humble beginnings. It is fair to say that he grew up in poverty. During his childhood he would work long hours with his father in the restaurant. My father, however, was a genius and he excelled in his exams at school. Being from a family with limited financial means, his parents were unable to pay for the tuition fees for medical school despite my dad securing the necessary grades. He was, however, able to obtain a scholarship from the Egyptian Government to study medicine in Cairo University, one of the most prestigious universities in the region, certainly at the time. The President of Egypt was the charismatic Jamal Abdel Nasser who had a vision that there would be unity in the Arab world. Nasser had set up a foundation for brilliant Arab youth to apply for scholarships to study at prestigious universities in Egypt. My father qualified. To this day, my father's clinic in Lebanon is full of pictures of Jamal Abdel Nasser, such is the immense gratitude my father has towards the Egyptian nationalist for the pivotal role the premier played in my father's life, and indeed my life. Otherwise, my father would never have broken the intergenerational poverty cycle and my fate would have turned out to be very different.

My father qualified as a physician in the early 1980s when the Lebanon–Israel war was still raging. It was a brutal and bloody war that had devastating consequences. The conflict captured the attention of international media outlets. I think this was in part because of the presence of the Multinational Force (MNF) including the US military. The decision to deploy troops to Lebanon may perhaps be one of the US Government's deepest regrets.

On 23 August 1983, early on a Sunday morning, trucks loaded with bombs were driven into buildings at the US Marine Corps barracks and were detonated. The suicide attack killed 307 people including 241 US military personnel. The 1983 Beirut barracks bombings resulted in the largest single day death toll for the US Armed Forces since the Vietnam War. I have no recollection of this as I was an infant at the time. But what I do have memories of were how the brutality of the Lebanon war seeped into popular culture. I remember, for example, the British band Human League and their single, 'The Lebanon' being played by radio stations in the 1980s and 1990s. The lyrics continue to haunt me to this day.

The Lebanon–Israel war and its consequences were major factors that influenced my dad's decision to migrate to Northern Ireland where another conflict was taking place, 'The Troubles'. However, just before he left Lebanon behind, he met my mother in a village. He, a dashing doctor, my mum a beautiful belle, they did not waste any time before exchanging vows and getting married. Together they travelled to Belfast where my father worked as an obstetrician. The situation in Belfast back then was far from stable. My mother would always say to me, 'Son, it was like jumping out of the frying pan and into the fire!' Indeed, Belfast at the time was considered one of the most dangerous cities in the world. I remember recently being interviewed by a radio talk show host after posting a comment on social media about obtaining my Certificate of Completion of Specialist Training and becoming a Consultant Psychiatrist. He wanted to know about my background so I told him that I was born in Belfast. After goading me for more information, I proceeded to share with him what my mother had said to me in relation to the advance alerts that they would receive that a bomb would be detonated at a particular time and place. At this point, the host excitedly revealed that he himself hails from that region of Ireland. He then added, 'Yes, what you describe were the infamous notifications that the IRA used to issue.'

I was born against this backdrop of civil strife in Belfast in 1982. The territory at the time was being disputed; was Northern Ireland (or is it the northern part of the island of Ireland?) part of the United Kingdom or was it part of a United Ireland? Irrespective of political persuasion and ideology, I received both British and Irish nationalities. This is tremendously beneficial as I remain a citizen of the European Union following Brexit and I receive all the advantages associated with this! My twin brother, for example, has been living in Germany for the past decade and he has experienced firsthand the benefits of being an Irish national in Europe following Brexit as it was a lot easier for him to work there compared to his British counterparts.

I don't remember Belfast. My parents moved to Dublin a couple of years after my father secured work in the Coombe Hospital as an obstetrician delivering babies, performing C-sections and carrying out other surgical procedures. However, that is not to say Belfast doesn't have any influence on my identity. I returned to Belfast for the first time since leaving in 2019 just before the first wave of the pandemic. I was invited by Queen's

University to deliver a talk about tackling mental-health-related stigma in medical students and doctors. BBC Radio Ulster soon caught wind and the following morning I found myself in their studio. I felt a deep, sincere and authentic connection with the talk show host as I almost always do with Irish people. I can't fully explain why but my being born there and feeling accepted as Irish I think certainly plays a role. During my interview I signposted my journey but we also spoke about how Northern Ireland has the highest rates of suicide in the United Kingdom. The authors of the paper that was published in The Lancet Psychiatry report that the trauma from The Troubles was transmitted throughout the generations and it is a factor that contributed to suicide in Northern Ireland. The authors therefore urgently recommend that more trauma-informed care must be made available to help heal the psychological wounds sustained as a result of The Troubles.

My parents, like many other people who migrate, seek asylum or sanctuary, didn't relocate because they wanted to but because the devastating consequences of conflict left them with no other choice. The mental health of this population often falls under the purview of cultural psychiatry for which there is a growing body of research evidence. The data does indicate that being a migrant, asylum seeker or refugee can increase your risk of developing mental health problems. Multiple factors contribute to this such as how we are received by the host country, language barriers, employment opportunities and housing insecurity. Interestingly, second-generation immigrants are at higher risk of developing psychosis compared to first-generation immigrants. I would hypothesise that the former have more difficulties grappling with identity than the latter. We all long to belong but for second-generation immigrants it seems, certainly to me, that we struggle with knowing who we are and which tribe we are a member of. My twin brother said something to me once that I'll never forget. He said that although we are British nationals, it felt as though we were never treated or accepted as such, certainly not by the community we were immersed in when we returned to England in 2000. This despite our best efforts to integrate and the fact that we identified strongly as British. This identity crisis, certainly for me, precipitated emotional turmoil and rendered me vulnerable to developing mental health problems in the future.

It seemed to me that the prevailing culture in England was to drink alcohol. For you to be accepted and embraced as 'one of our own' one must subscribe to this culture. Being a Muslim, therefore, didn't stand me in good stead for social inclusion since consuming intoxicants is haram (prohibited) in Islam. I think this only served to alienate me and no doubt many other teetotallers from full social acceptance, which further increased our risk of developing mental health problems.

The rhetoric being espoused by certain politicians about immigration and seeking asylum and the policies, both those being proposed and those that are already implemented, undoubtedly has adverse effects on the mental health of those being targeted. Britain's Home Secretary Suella Braverman has come under scrutiny and criticism for the language she has been using when she is describing migrants and people who seek sanctuary. When dehumanising terms are used to describe a people it can have disastrous effects on our mental health.

One of the most striking policies against people seeking sanctuary was when Donald Trump was in office and he issued an Executive Order that resulted in the forced separation of children from their parents often for protracted periods. Such forced separation can cause irreparable damage to the mental health of both children and parents and, certainly for me, is unconscionable.

Discussions about immigration and seeking sanctuary are often in the context of the Global North. However, we know most people receive refuge and sanctuary in low- and middle-income countries like Lebanon. Indeed, up to one-in-four people in Lebanon is from Syria or Palestine. Refugees in Lebanon are often deprived of healthcare and doctors would turn them away if they did not have the resources to pay.

My father Dr Zakaria Hankir, however, was the exception. The Arabic word for doctor is 'Hakeem', which means 'The wise one.' I used to shadow my father in his clinic in Sidon, which is the capital of the south of Lebanon. What I witnessed in that clinic astonished and inspired me. In Lebanon, unlike the United Kingdom, there is no universal healthcare, and the poor would bear the brunt of this. However, my father would provide pro bono care to those who could not afford it, and he was affectionately known as 'Hakeem el-shaab' or

'The People's Doctor'. His clinic would be packed with patients from lower socioeconomic backgrounds, many Palestinian and Syrian refugees who were regarded as outcasts and who were some of the most vulnerable people in Lebanese society. I remember many of my father's patients would be dressed in tattered attire covered in dust after walking for miles (some for an entire day) to get to the clinic, the blisters on their feet testament to how arduous their journeys were.

Despite my father's valiant efforts, the physical health treatment gap in Lebanon for refugees remains enormous. The gap, however, is even greater for the treatment of mental health conditions. Indeed, the provision of mental healthcare for refugees in Lebanon is close to non-existent.

In this chapter, I have briefly traced my parents' journeys to illustrate the profound influences their life events have had on my own life and trajectory. Much of what happens to us is beyond our control and events that occur even before we are born can place us in disadvantageous circumstances. We often have no power or say over the factors that can increase our risk towards or protect us against developing mental health problems. Migration, conflict, racism, politics and how we are received by the host nation are but some of the myriad factors that can contribute to developing mental health conditions. Immigrants and those of us who seek sanctuary are often stigmatised and socially excluded. We can struggle with identity formation, which can further render us vulnerable to developing mental health problems. Although much of the discourse on asylum seekers and refugees in the international media seems focused on events in the Global North, most asylum seekers and refugees are based in low- and middle-income countries like Lebanon. The provision of healthcare – especially mental health care – for this population in these parts of the world is woefully inadequate. This is deeply concerning especially given the complex mental health needs of this population. Solutions to these problems require political will on a global scale and the mobilisation of resources to fund mental healthcare provision that is grounded on a human rights framework and that is trauma informed. You as an individual can feel powerless but you can make a difference. Simply by being kind and by opening our hearts and minds to people who migrate and who are forced to seek sanctuary can contribute to creating a compassionate culture and atmosphere. This can help to make immigrants and those who seek sanctuary feel accepted, included, welcomed and even embraced, the mental health benefits of which cannot be overstated. I know that if I was made to feel 'embraced' when I arrived in the United Kingdom all those years ago, that would certainly have been beneficial for my mental health. Unfortunately, as will be revealed in this book, I was often alienated and made to feel unwelcome by many, which had profoundly adverse effects on my mental health.

2

Identity Formation and Fragmentation

I don't remember having any negative experiences in Dublin. I can only recall green and expansive fields as far as the eye can see and friendly people who would always return a smile and exchange greetings with me. Of course, you see the world through a very different lens when you are a child but the point remains I had a happy childhood growing up in Ireland. I remember school being fun and I was always, without exception, accepted by my peers. I certainly don't remember any adverse childhood experiences. Not because my mind has repressed or suppressed them. But because this period of my life was relatively 'normal'. I wasn't the outlier. It also helped that my father was seemingly comfortable with finances. The fridge was always full of fresh food and the house we lived in had a massive back garden. The area felt safe and secure. Life wasn't tainted by trauma back then, certainly not consciously.

I do, however, recollect my mother crying to herself from time to time with a cup of coffee in her hands and rocking back and forth. Leaving her family behind in Lebanon and migrating to Ireland with my father was deeply distressing. She also had to raise five children more or less single handedly given that my father would spend long hours working in the hospital. Mum had such a close bond with her parents and siblings. They all grew up together on a farm where my grandfather would harvest the fruits. The scent of jasmine would permeate the Mediterranean breeze (mum even named my youngest sister Jasmine, such was the nostalgic effect that this flower's aroma would have on her).

This was in the 1980s before the advent of the digital age. There was no such thing as WhatsApp or FaceTime. For my grandparents to call my mother they would have to travel to Sidon from the farm they lived on which was at least a 30-minute drive to a place where you could make international phone calls. The costs were prohibitively substantial so these calls were unfortunately rare. I remember the phone ringing and my mother picking up. There would be a delay and instantly the expression on her face transformed into excitement. She would switch from English to Arabic when she realised she was receiving an international call from her parents in Lebanon. I could hear her shouting because the connection was so poor. These conversations never lasted long enough and just when she got into the rhythm of talking and you could see her smiling and laughing the call ended abruptly for my grandparents ran out of credit. My mother of course would cling onto the hope that the reception was poor and that she just had to wait a moment to hear their voices again. But as soon as reality sank in her face turned sombre and she would place the phone back on the receiver. She would then withdraw into herself and cry inconsolably. My mum was understandably depressed during my childhood. I mean, who wouldn't be in her circumstances? All alone in an alien world.

I will never forget traveling to Lebanon with my mother during this period. She wanted to pay my grandparents a surprise visit. It was raining in the village where they lived. There is a relatively long drive that traversed the farm before you would arrive at my grandparents' house. I remember the taxi driver flashing his lights and sounding the horn as he turned into the drive. My aunties would leave the house despite the rain to see what all the commotion was about. They had a suspicion that something exciting was happening, that my mother was paying them a surprise visit perhaps! The moment my grandfather caught onto this, he burst out of the house barefoot and ran to the taxi, which would stop in the middle of the drive, rain pouring all over him. My mother would emerge from the car and even though it was raining, I could still see the tears of joy streaming down their faces as they hugged each other tightly. I remember my grandfather crying, his eyes were red because of all the tears. He would incessantly kiss my mother on her forehead and repeatedly say to her 'habibti, habibti', 'my sweetheart, my sweetheart' with paternal love and affection. Just remembering this moment makes my eyes well up. I can't begin to fathom the pain that it must have caused my mother to have been separated from my grandfather when she left him to move to Ireland.

Clinical depression or major depressive disorder were not in my repertoire of words back then. I am fairly certain mum would have met all the diagnostic criteria. Sadness was, however, in my vocabulary and I remember my mum being sad. But I also remember her being happy. For example, I think the local community was excited that there was a Lebanese family in town and that someone might be able to cook some delicious Lebanese cuisine! We would have guests come over including my school teachers. It sounded like a commotion emerging from the dining room when the food was being served! My mother even published a small Lebanese cookbook, which was hugely popular amongst the locals. I think now about how activities like cooking can be protective for our mental health. This preoccupation can give you a sense of purpose and pride through inviting people over to share the mouthwatering meals with; culinary skills can also promote social connectedness and community cohesion. Maybe cooking for her family and others, as a hobby and of her own volition, was a factor that prevented my mother's mental health from deteriorating even further, heaven forbid, into a severe depressive episode with psychotic symptoms.

Notwithstanding my mother's struggles, life in Ireland, for the most part and certainly for me but of course not for everyone, was like a dream. It was only when we moved to England after my father was offered a job that we noticed our skin complexion wasn't white. I lost count how many times the other pupils at the school we attended would make racial taunts at us. It was not uncommon to get into scraps. Although I had a strong aversion towards any type of violence I had no other option but to defend myself. I'll never forget one day a group of boys yelling at us from a distance and calling us derogatory names. One of them launched a stone at us and narrowly missed. I admired how my older brother was not intimated, however, I was surprised when he suddenly and fearlessly picked the stone from off the ground and hurled it back at them. I thought that was the end of that but suddenly and seemingly from out of nowhere one of the boys ran as fast as he could towards my brother and with full force and momentum he swung a metal tennis racket at the back of my brother's head. Blood immediately started gushing out and I was left in a state of shock. Having worked as a doctor in emergency medicine for five years, I know now that such a blow to the head could quite easily have caused an intra-cranial bleed and killed him. My brother, however, wasn't perturbed in the slightest. He didn't even flinch. All he did was slowly and gently place his hand on the back of his head as if to assess the damage. He then applied pressure to the wound and resumed his walk as if nothing had happened. To this day I think where did the hatred that fuelled this violent attack come from? How could a person, no less a child, just assault another person, a fellow child, without a trace of compunction, hesitation or restraint?

'You will never be one of them' my dad's best friend would say to us when we were children. As if to labour the point he then said, 'What do they call you, Paki!' It is a disgusting term that betrays the racist attitude towards people who are brown in colour. Of course, you don't have to be from Pakistan to be called a Paki in the same way that you don't have to be a Muslim to be a victim of Islamophobia. Ask members of the Sikh community; many of them have been victims of Islamophobic attacks (more on that later). When I returned to England from Lebanon (we moved to Leeds in 2000) I remember a racist incident that was covered by the media involving a professional football player for Leeds United Football Club. He was being served a meal in a fast food restaurant and he said to the cashier, 'I don't want no Paki serving me chips' when alluding to the cashier's colleague. Such flippant and offhand remarks do reveal an underlying racism that is deeply entrenched that can be very harmful to recipients. This is all the more concerning when you are a footballer because you are idolised and you have tremendous influence. Of course, that is not to say that there aren't any kind and compassionate people who are welcoming and accepting towards immigrants. But to say racism doesn't exist, especially in its more subtle and indirect forms or to dismiss attacks, attitudes and comments as not being racist simply isn't true. Often the victim is framed as being sensitive and the fault is with them and how they construed the words and actions. I can share an astonishing anecdote to illustrate the point. This is a true story that occurred when I was a student in a secondary school in Worcester, which is in the Midlands of England. A fellow student reported to his teacher that a peer of his referred to him as a Paki. Instead of validating the racial attack and condemning it and summoning the perpetrator and comforting the child, the teacher in a very nonchalant and matter of fact manner replied, 'But you are a Paki' as if the term was not derogatory and was not uttered with the intention to offend or to insult but merely to denote his ancestry is in Pakistan. This gaslighting came from an authority figure like a teacher! To this day that memory still upsets and unsettles me.

The Premier League in England has launched an anti-racism campaign #noroomforracism in attempts to stamp out this form of hatred in football stadiums, online and beyond. Footballers of colour continue to bear the brunt of racial slurs that can be deeply wounding. In the 2020 UEFA European Football Championship (which took place in 2021 due to the pandemic) when England reached the finals they were pitted against Italy. After full time and extra time there was a deadlock so there had to be a penalty shootout, which England lost. The England internationals who missed their penalties were men of colour and the racism they were subjected to, especially online and on social media, was abhorrent. It's as if we will only accept you as English and 'one of our own' if you score goals and win. Of course, England is far from unique in this regard. Professional players of colour in France and other countries are also subjected to a torrent of racial abuse if the score line doesn't go their way. And these are professional footballers! What's it like for the average Afzal stacking shelves on minimum wage?

Maybe my dad's best friend was right? Maybe we will never be fully accepted in British society because of the complexion of our skin, our Muslim names and our background. Perhaps it was time for my parents to reevaluate their options? My father was not exempt from racial discrimination in the workplace. That, coupled with my mother's homesickness, compelled them to make the difficult decision to return to Lebanon. So, the family packed our bags and we moved to the Middle East. I remember resenting my parents. Although at that age I wasn't denying or rejecting my Lebanese background, I very much identified as English despite the racism I experienced.

Having completed his specialist training in Ireland and the United Kingdom my father could be excused for thinking that this might increase his employability and that he might be able to secure one of the few high paying jobs in one of the more prestigious hospitals. Our disappointment, however, was as great as our hopes were high. The medical profession in Lebanon is based on a structure that places more importance on who you know (not what you know). Reputation (i.e., are you a well-known, highly respected and trusted individual in society) also played a part in how many patients attended your clinic. Having been absent from the country for 16 years few people knew who my father was despite his expertise and vast experience as a doctor. This had a profound effect on his clinical practice and the number of paying patients he assessed and treated in his clinic. This ultimately affected the amount of revenue my father was able to generate from work, certainly initially. Like many, many other families in Lebanon at the time (the aftermath of the civil war, more about this below) we experienced financial hardship. However, despite this, it was during this period in my life that I had my happiest experiences. This was because this period was before the devastating fragmentation of my family. Suffice to say having a robust family structure to a degree was a buffer against the harmful effects of poverty.

Outside the family home, Lebanon was a traumatised nation. The legacy of the infamous Sabra and Shatila massacres – that involved up to 3500 civilians who were mostly Palestinian and Lebanese Shiites – was of division along sectarian lines and it continued to influence social and political structures in the region. Indeed, the political structure in Lebanon was configured on confessionalism whereby the Speaker of The House is Shiite, the Prime Minister is Sunni and the President is Christian.

It behoves me to, at the very least, briefly describe the massacres that took place in the Sabra and Shatila refugee camps in Beirut not least because that event should never be erased from the history books and our collective consciousness. The victims deserve more than that and they should never be forgotten. 'The Nakba' or 'The Catastrophe' resulted in a large Palestinian influx and presence in Lebanon. Moreover, during the civil war in the 1980s members of the Palestine Liberation Organization (PLO), led by Yasser Arafat, were fleeing into Lebanon. The Israeli Defense Forces (IDF) invaded Lebanon in the early 1980s, a path of destruction in their wake. My maternal uncle shared a story with me when I was an adolescent living in Lebanon that I'll never forget. Back in the day, Khaloo (the Arabic term for maternal uncle) used to own a sky-blue Honda Civic. At the time, there was only one main road connecting the south of Lebanon to the capital Beirut. Israeli warships would occupy Lebanese territorial waters. My uncle would say, he used to put his car radio on full blast (usually a ballad from Guns and Roses) and with his foot all the way down on the pedal he would speed down the highway whilst the warship would take aim at vehicles and fire.

Alliances between the warring parties and political factions were in a state of flux and constantly shifting in Lebanon. One of the most powerful political parties at the time was the Kataeb (also known as the Phalange), and Bachir Gemayel was their charismatic leader. Bachir was later elected President of Lebanon during the civil war in 1982. He became the supreme commander of the Lebanese Forces, uniting major Christian militias by force under the slogan of 'Uniting the Christian Rifle'. Gemayel and his party formed an alliance with Israel who were united in their fight against the PLO. Gemayel is regarded as an icon and one of the most controversial figures in Lebanon. A leader who exuded panache, he was adulated and adored by his followers, especially by the Maronite Christians. However, his detractors accused him of treason for his relationship with Israel 'the enemy'. On 14 September 1982, a day before my birth in Belfast, whilst Gemayel was giving an address to his fellow Phalangists in their headquarters in Achrafieh in east Beirut, a bomb was detonated. Gemayel had been assassinated. Perhaps because of the love that his followers had for him, rumours had spread that Gemayel had somehow survived the explosion and phalangists clung to this hope. However, his death was confirmed and announced to the outcry of his followers.

Waltz with Bashir is a 2008 Israeli animated documentary film written and directed by Ari Folman. It portrays the protagonist (Folman) in search of his lost memories of his experiences as a soldier in the 1982 Lebanon War and his attempt to both decipher them and reconcile himself with them. It vividly depicts the massacres of Palestinians in the Sabra and Shatila refugee camps in Beirut through the lens of an IDF veteran and the harrowing effects that post-traumatic stress disorder (PTSD) has on him. *Waltz with Bashir* was nominated for an Academy Award for Best Foreign Language Film. However, despite its popularity and critical acclaim it is officially banned in Lebanon. A character in the film, an IDF veteran who also fought in the 1982 Lebanon War, narrates to Folman that following Gemayel's assassination he had a terrible foreboding that something perverse was about to happen in retaliation and to avenge the leader of the Kataeb party's death. Tragically, the foreboding materialised : a few days later the massacres of Sabra and Shatila took place during which up to 3500 people were killed. The perpetrators were reportedly the Maronite Christian militia branch of the Lebanese Forces. The IDF had invaded Lebanon 'to root out the PLO' and there were reports that despite their presence and awareness that a massacre was unfolding in the camps, they did not take any action to prevent and stop it from taking place.

The atrocities that occurred in the refugee camps are unspeakable. Human beings – young and old, men, women and children alike – were slaughtered, tortured and mutilated. I can't even begin to imagine the psychological consequences and the traumatic effects that such horrifying events can have on the minds of all those affected. No amount of therapy will heal the psychological wounds that were sustained as a result of the massacre. The perpetrators, whoever they were, seemingly evaded accountability. Without accountability, the trauma will remain unresolved. Even with accountability, that will never bring back the loved ones who were mercilessly and heartlessly killed. Generations later, memories of those dark days continue to haunt all who were involved adversely affecting their mental health: the Lebanese, Palestinians and the Israelis who were occupying Lebanon.

The formative years (or, as I would call them, 'The Wonder Years') was a fascinating period in my life. I initially was unable to speak Arabic at the time and I very much felt like an 'outsider'. The native Lebanese people would even call us ajnabi, which is Arabic for foreigner or stranger, when they discovered that we were not proficient in the Arabic language and that we were born and raised in Ireland and the United Kingdom, respectively. There were no secondary schools that had a UK curriculum that my parents could find so they enrolled us into a secondary school that had an US curriculum (the Lebanese American School), and this is when I first heard the US accent, which at the time was incomprehensible to me (and I'm sure my UK accent was incomprehensible to them!). Although the school was American it was really a melting pot. There were pupils from all over the world including Australia, Colombia, Venezuela,

Canada, Brazil and Sierra Leone. We didn't have many students from Lebanon who lived outside Lebanon. They were the minority and yes, I would even say stigmatised. I soon learned about 'forbidden love'. In Islam, a man is permitted to marry a 'person from the book' (i.e., Christian or Jew), providing that the children are raised as Muslim. Bearing in mind that Lebanon was brutalised by a devastating civil war, this added another dimension to interfaith relationships and to broken hearts since this barrier commonly prevented a Muslim lady from marrying a Christian man (such people would populate the clinics of psychologists and psychiatrists in Beirut).

Was this spell in Lebanon the happiest years of my life? Maybe. I can't put it into words. I just remember having so much fun! The Americans in particular really knew how to enjoy themselves! They were so extroverted and gregarious. The Latin Americans were so warm and sincere. The Aussies were an interesting bunch too! Full of character and zest. They would often make fun of us 'Brits'! Our family was the only one from England as far as I can remember. But that didn't intimidate me in the slightest. On the contrary, as far as I was concerned, the only country that mattered was England, and the capital of the world was London! I always had this sense if not yearning that we would return.

Initially, I was reluctant to socialise with the other students but instead decided to retreat into my books. I would study throughout the night and for the entire weekend. My hard work and discipline paid off and I excelled scholastically, especially in mathematics.

I would frequently receive the highest grades in all subjects in the class as evidenced in our report cards that would be announced every month. This would be a source of shame and embarrassment or pride and joy depending on your grades. The students who were struggling with their exams, the popular ones from the capital Beirut, would befriend me and in their attempts to appease their parents they would often invite me to their homes for sleepovers during which I would be their personal tutor. I enjoyed being a hit with the parents as they would frequently heap praise upon me!

Slowly but surely, I started to integrate with my peers, especially the Americans. I acquired an obsession for basketball despite being 'vertically challenged'. An obsession it was though and I simply couldn't stop playing basketball whenever the opportunity arose. Eat, drink and sleep basketball. Repeat. I can see now that what was driving me back then, as what drives me now, was defiance. That is to say, a resolute refusal to accept that I didn't have what it takes to be the best basketball player. The reality was that I was talented to a degree but I was always limited. Not only by my height but by ability. At the time I was blinded by my determination to succeed in basketball and to prove the naysayers wrong, even to my own detriment. I continued to excel in my exams, but my academic performance wasn't as brilliant as it was before my obsession with basketball.

My obsession with basketball helped me to become increasingly socially active even in my hometown of Sidon. Whenever there was an opportunity to play I seized it. My Arabic started to improve as I mingled more with the locals. Being the 'ajnabi' conferred to a degree some celebrity status! One day my father received a phone call (this was way before the ubiquity of the smartphone and I didn't have my own mobile) from the Prime Minister's nephew Ahmed Hariri who was a native of Sidon. It turned out Ahmed heard about me and he too was obsessed with basketball! Next thing I knew, his bodyguard showed up outside our apartment in a 4 x 4 Range Rover and I was driven to the Prime Minister's sister's mansion, which was majestic! The Prime Minister Rafic Hariri (also known as Mr Lebanon) was a self-made billionaire and the Hariri family name was one of the most respectable and powerful in Lebanon. Despite his fame and fortune, Ahmed was humble, kind, caring and sincere. We soon became very close friends. Even to this day we remain in touch despite the heavy demands his hectic political career places upon him.

Locals were intrigued and they wanted to know what it was like living abroad, I think in part because they had fantasies of one day escaping from Lebanon and living better lives. I revelled in the attention but I wanted to remain grounded and, most importantly for me, have a strong connection with the Islamic faith that emphasised the values of humility and being kind and friendly to all, irrespective of wealth or class. Society in Sidon, much like the rest of Lebanon, was heavily influenced by class and wealth. I refused to subscribe to this. It didn't matter to me how well off your family was, how big your house was or how fast your car was. What mattered to me were the values of kindness, sincerity and humility.

To this day these universal values continue to inform and guide my approach to life.

Like all things in life, good and bad, the wonder years had to come to an end. However, it did so in spectacular fashion. I graduated top of the class at high school and I received a plaque to commemorate this at a ceremony that was attended by politicians and dignitaries. During the photoshoot with the principal of the school draped in regalia I was presented with the plaque. At that moment I felt anything was possible and that I could realise even my wildest dreams. It was an exhilarating and enlightening high. Not in the psychopathological 'manic' sense for my mood was 'congruent' and consistent with my circumstances and reality. Little did I know then that I would come crashing down and that my reality and circumstances would change dramatically. . ..

3
Disillusionment

Just when I felt like I was settling down in Lebanon, the time had come for me to return to the United Kingdom. I had only lived in 'the Levant' for five years, however, it felt like I had lived there an entire lifetime. I think, as I mentioned in the previous chapter, the fact that I was there during my formative years influences this perception. I don't ever remember having a choice to leave my parents behind in Lebanon. It always felt like leaving was the only option. I was 17 years old at the time. I was still very much beholden to my parents. All I understood was that my parents knew what was best for me and that they had my best interests in their hearts. Remaining in Lebanon was not an option or so I was led to believe. I think the main issue was that my father, like many other fathers in Lebanon, couldn't afford to pay for me, and my twin brother, to go to university. The remuneration he received was not a reflection of all of his hard work. Also, it didn't make sense to stay in Lebanon when we had the chance to go to the United Kingdom. Lebanon was a developing nation, the

United Kingdom a developed nation. Opportunities in Lebanon were limited whereas in the United Kingdom they were plentiful. In fact, money grows on trees in the United Kingdom!

It was a no-brainer. We were extremely fortunate and blessed to have the opportunity to go to the United Kingdom. People in Lebanon would literally kill to have the opportunity that we did. We also had British passports. There was no further consideration. As British nationals, we would be taken care of (presumably by the British Government) and we would be valued, embraced, supported and loved. Everything would be sorted and everything would be okay. It was a done deal. We had everything to be optimistic and excited about.

However, that wasn't the feeling I remember experiencing when we were in Beirut International Airport. I remember my sisters were there and my younger brother and my parents. I remember looking back as I was walking towards passport control and seeing my father with his hands in his pockets looking sombre and serious and my mum blowing us kisses and saying that she loved us. And that was it. I could no longer see or hear my family. I just remember the official at passport control asking us for our travel documents. We started a friendly conversation in the English language. Initially, he was all smiles but suddenly there was a scare. He called out to his colleague and shouted in Arabic 'are we taking 82 in?' To which his colleague (and to our immense and immediate relief) casually replied in Arabic, 'No, no'.

Military conscription in Lebanon was still mandatory. By the time you turned 18, all men were expected to complete one year of military service. There were some exceptions for certain health conditions or if you were the only son ('waheed') in the family (the 'shabab' or lads in Lebanon would be envious about this when they found out if one of us was 'waheed' since we weren't too enthusiastic about joining the military. If anything, many of us would do anything we could to get ourselves out of that situation).

When the official at passport control called out to his colleague asking if they were 'taking in 82' he was referring to our year of birth. The date that I left my parents will forever be etched in my mind: 10 July 2000. This was just shy of my 18th birthday. My brother and I made a narrow escape. He stamped our passports and before we knew it, we were on the plane to England.

A few hours into the flight I noticed Mohammed was tearful. I asked him why he was crying, but I already knew the answer. We had just left everything that we knew and that mattered to us behind. For some reason, I didn't shed a tear. I didn't even feel sad. Was I in denial of my reality? Maybe I was. We arrived at Heathrow Airport in London. I can't take for granted being able to enter the United Kingdom so easily. I didn't have to risk my life and take a perilous journey. But just because I wasn't a refugee, it didn't mean life was a walk in the park for me. On the contrary, life felt more like an impossible mission at times. And not all people who seek sanctuary or refuge are refugees. In a sense, I was seeking sanctuary from the precarious situation in Lebanon.

We collected all our worldly possessions from the conveyor belt, which were in two suitcases, and began our journey to Worcester, where my older brother Khodor lived. Khodor, like the men of the family were all expected to do, had travelled to England a year before us. Khodor deserves an entire book in his own right. The suffering and struggling that he went through to soften the landing for us was immense.

Khodor was with his friend, a refugee from Chechnya called Mehmet who kindly collected us and drove us to Khodor's room. Looking back now, I just don't think we were able to process the enormity of what was happening to us. We effectively left our parents behind us at 17 years of age and we had no idea what lay ahead of us. We only knew that we had to find work as quickly as possible. Our father had given us a small amount of money but we all knew that wouldn't last for long.

On Khodor's advice, we decided that we would move to Leeds. It was a bigger and more diverse city than Worcester. Khodor had been the victim of multiple racist incidents including several stop-and-searches by the police for no valid reason other than him being a man of colour. The British Defence League also approached him 'ordering' him to leave 'their' country. I remember Khodor being so traumatised that he spoke very little. He didn't want what happened to him in Worcester to happen to us. We also had our best childhood friend

Wassim living in Leeds. His mother in fact went to the same school in Sidon as my mother did and they, too, were close friends.

The plan was for Khodor and Mohammed to go to Leeds first and I would follow them. I volunteered to stay behind to help Mehmet out. Every weekend Mehmet would go to Malvern Hills where there was a kebab van. So that weekend, I decided to join him.

I remember the darkness as we drove towards the battered kebab van. After several attempts to get it started we drove to the pubs – the best place for selling kebabs and burgers! I was, in fact, very enthusiastic to get started. Plus, this was just temporary and a means to an end, right? I'll be in medical school in no time and I'll realise my dream to become a doctor. This was my first paying job and I got to work with gusto. The customers were mostly polite. I remember one customer asking me if I could speak English. It didn't really bother me so much at the time. If anything, I think I found it quite amusing. I was confident in my intellectual abilities and in my mind, I was thinking 'I've fooled them, haven't I!'

As we went deeper into the night it became increasingly busy with customers. Whilst I was flipping burgers there was suddenly a commotion outside. Approximately 20 metres away from the van I could see a group of men who looked like they were in their early 20s. I couldn't believe the violence that unfolded. Together they were relentlessly stomping the head of a defenceless man on the ground. They were wearing boots. The stomping didn't stop and they were doing it with full force. The man didn't resist. He just lay on the ground motionless. His body and head would only move after every stomp. This must have lasted for 5 minutes but it felt like an eternity. The most astonishing thing about the scenario is that nobody intervened. Everybody just stood there and watched the brutality happen.

I couldn't just be a bystander, I had to do something. But Mehmet grabbed hold of my arm and sternly commanded me to remain where I was. We were the only visible ethnics in the vicinity. He knew full well that we were vulnerable prey to these predators who were clearly intoxicated. And so, I did as I was told. They eventually stopped, I think partly out of exhaustion. I don't think they felt guilty in the slightest. I think they realised that the police had been called because we could hear sirens in the distance. Once they disappeared, a bystander approached the motionless victim and attempted to resuscitate him. I was shocked when other bystanders tried to stop him and accused him of trying to be heroic. He was just being humane after witnessing an episode of inhumanity. The police and paramedics eventually arrived, and the victim was taken away.

The police obtained a witness statement from my boss whilst I resumed my duties in the van. I don't remember giving it further consideration at the time. I don't remember being afraid. I think my way of coping with the incident was to just block it out and act as if it never happened. The following few days the site swarmed with police. Other customers said they heard the man had died. I don't know if this was true or not, but it wouldn't surprise me if it was, given the ferocity of the attack and how long it lasted.

I lived in Lebanon during the Qana massacre in 1996 when the IDF fired artillery shells at a United Nations (UN) compound. Of the 800 Lebanese civilians who had taken refuge in the compound, 106 were killed and approximately 116 injured. The attack occurred amid heavy fighting between the IDF and Hezbollah during Operation Grapes of Wrath. It was during this time that I saw something that I will never forget. A father had left his family behind in his home briefly to fetch some water. During his absence there was an air raid by Israeli military jets. When he returned, he discovered that his home had been bombed and reduced to rubble. His family had been killed. I remember him holding his child's dead body in his arms and crying to God. He wasn't wailing hysterically. But his crying still penetrated my soul. I think he was blaming himself for what had happened and consumed by remorse, he was begging to his deceased family and to God to forgive him for failing to uphold his duty as a father to protect.

I witnessed his reaction to his family's death live on national television. But that was different. The killing of the man in Malvern Hills was the first death I had witnessed in person with the naked eye. I was 17 years old and I had seen something that no one should ever have to see, let alone an adolescent. I got paid £40 for three, back-to-back, 12-hour night shifts selling burgers and kebabs. I didn't complain. In fact, it was the most money I had ever made in my entire life. It felt like I hit the jackpot. On Monday, I packed my bags, bade farewell to Worcester and made my way to Leeds to meet my brothers and my best friend.

I remember meeting my brothers and best friend Wassim at Leeds Bus Station. Wassim had a huge smile on his face and he was very happy to see me. I was very happy to see him too. We had last seen each other in Lebanon many years ago. He greeted me warmly and we embraced each other. Khodor managed to find a house for us all to live in. It was in an area called Chapeltown. The rent was a lot cheaper than in other areas. It should have occurred to us why but it didn't. I would later learn that Chapeltown was one of the rougher areas in Leeds, if not the roughest. Signs of poverty and neglect by the local council were ubiquitous. Houses and streets were in states of disrepair. Litter covered the sidewalks and roads. I wish I could say I couldn't smell the scent of cannabis in the air, but that wouldn't be true. But we were nonetheless immensely grateful. We had found a home and even then at that young age we knew not to take that for granted. Housing insecurity is a huge unresolved issue even in a 'developed nation' like the United Kingdom. I would later see in my clinical practice as a doctor working in Emergency Psychiatry how adversely home insecurity and homelessness would affect mental health.

The next day I went job hunting. The local Job Centre would advertise vacancies and I would apply. I was 17;

the only work experience I had was in the kebab van in Malvern Hills. Applications for the higher paying jobs would get rejected almost immediately. The only job I could secure was working as a janitor in C&A, which was a department store that was shutting down. Needless to say it paid minimum wage which at the time was £4/hour. It's difficult for me to write about this experience. I think I was naive and oblivious to social dynamics and societal structures grounded on class. I wish I could say it didn't matter what kind of occupation or wealth you had, and that people will treat you the same irrespective of your socioeconomic status. The reality was that these things did matter and I learned the hard way.

I remember being in high spirits and saying good morning to C&A staff members who were huddled outside in a group waiting for the door to be unlocked. They would stare at me as if I was some weirdo. I think unconsciously I was trying to fill this huge void in my life. I had left all my friends and most of my family behind in Lebanon. But my colleagues at work weren't interested. I think I understand why to a degree. There was a clash of cultures. I think it's fair to say British culture is, generally speaking, more reserved. Lebanese culture, especially the culture in the American high school I graduated from in Lebanon, was more outgoing and would embrace extroverted and gregarious individuals. But I don't think it was just cultural. I was a 'lowly janitor'. That was, as far my colleagues were concerned, my class and social standing. And I don't think my ethnicity and faith made social integration any easier.

The job in C&A working as a janitor was only part time and didn't pay well. I needed to find another job to augment my income. So, I returned to the Job Centre where I met the loveliest lady who was a member of staff. She had a strong Yorkshire accent and would often refer to me as 'luv', which I later learned was not uncommon in Leeds! 'Luv' was an affectionate colloquialism, something that I was desperately lacking in my life since arriving in England. She was so kind, caring and maternal. She said something I'll never forget. When she found out that I excelled at school she quickly made the observation that I wasn't like the other people at the Job Centre. She looked around her, leaned forward and quietly whispered to me, 'Be careful, there are some rough people here.' Not in a judgemental way, but in a protective way. For whatever reason, most of the other people decided against going down the education route.

It almost felt like she was rapidly able to read and assess my situation. I didn't end up here because I flunked my exams or because I had a terrible attitude or because I lacked the ambition and discipline to get into university and succeed. It's like she was saying to me, 'What on Earth are you doing here?! You don't belong here. You shouldn't be here. Go to university and get yourself a degree and make something out of your life. You've got what it takes!'

Meanwhile, my hunt for another job wasn't going so well and I hit a brick wall. My applications kept on getting rejected, one after the other. But there was a separate application outside of the Job Centre that I had made to a department store called Marks & Spencer. The vacancy advertised was 'Stock Advisor' again on minimum wage. I had heard back from them but this time, my application wasn't rejected. I had been invited for an interview. I was over the moon! I attended the interview and, much like how I was towards the staff who worked in C&A, I was very outgoing and friendly. That was my character, my personality type. This time however, I received a warmer reaction. Not everyone could handle the excessive overtures but the reaction was definitely a lot more positive. The interview itself was pretty simple and straightforward. The job entailed stacking shelves, filling fridges and serving customers as a cashier, which I thought was easy enough. I thought I did okay for myself in the interview but they only offered me a temporary position, not a permanent one. I accepted their offer instantly. Before I knew it, I was dressed in the M&S uniform and I was unpacking boxes and placing the contents on the shop floor for customers to purchase.

I was extremely grateful to have a job irrespective of what type of work I was doing. Unemployment rates in Lebanon were very high and I lost count of how many despondent men I met in Lebanon who were desperate to find any type of work to support and feed their families. The responsibility was on them to provide and to protect. Relative to their situation, I was extremely blessed and fortunate. I remember a few years ago going to a takeaway in Thornton Heath, southeast London. It was late at night and this was after I finished a 12-hour shift working in Emergency Psychiatry. I started a conversation with the person working behind the till.

I said to him with empathy, remembering my personal experiences, that it must be tough. His response touched me. He didn't seem negative or bitter. On the contrary, he seemed immeasurably grateful and he said, 'Job. I have a job. I recently came here from India' and I got it. With all the job insecurity in the world, to have some form of employment isn't something we can ever take for granted. It wasn't something I was about to take for granted, that's for sure.

Notwithstanding my gratitude for finding work and for being able to work, I didn't leave my family behind in Lebanon to stack shelves, clean floors and fill fridges. Don't get me wrong, there is no shame in doing this and in fact I discharged my duties honourably and I was proud to earn an honest living. But the plan always was to get into medical school.

For as long as I can remember, I always wanted to be a doctor. Of course, there are the usual reasons: to make your parents proud, it's a respectable profession (if not the most highly respected), because you want to help people and so forth. This last reason, wanting to help people, is the one I think that shows up the most frequently on personal statements when applying to medical schools. It might sound disingenuous, but I genuinely wanted to help people. I witnessed suffering on a colossal scale in Lebanon and I felt duty-bound to help people who were less fortunate than me. So it made sense to want to become a doctor and choosing to study medicine at university was the natural choice. I didn't, however, always want to be a psychiatrist. In fact, that was probably the last branch of medicine that I wanted to specialise in. I think my views towards psychiatry and mental health before my episode of psychological distress when I was a medical student were shaped by my cultural background and, if I'm entirely honest, ignorance and yes even stigma. Mental health wasn't often spoken about back then, certainly not as much as it is now. And awareness about mental health in Lebanon was virtually non-existent. The only time mental health was ever brought up, was when labelling an individual as 'majnoon' or 'mad'. It was a deeply stigmatising and pejorative word. 'Mental illnesses' were not real illnesses and 'psychiatrists' were not real doctors. And I didn't think my father would be proud of his psychiatrist son. He certainly wouldn't show off to his doctor colleagues in hospitals in Sidon about his psychiatrist son! If I was to specialise in something, it would have to be plastic surgery or one of the more 'prestigious' specialties like cardiology. The die was cast long before I even enrolled in medical school: I was going to be a cardiothoracic or plastic surgeon or cardiologist but definitely not a psychiatrist.

There was this place in Leeds where you could go for advice about careers and education. So we went there to obtain advice in relation to our situation. As far as we were concerned and indeed led to believe by our parents in Lebanon, it would be a simple and straightforward affair: we would brandish our British passports and report cards and we would be granted immediate admission into medical school and we would also receive grants to fund living costs like rent.

This couldn't have been further from reality. It was true that we were British nationals, however, for us to be considered home students and to avoid paying international tuition fees, which were exorbitant and out of the question, we would have to have been resident, that is living in the United Kingdom for three consecutive years prior to starting university. Not only this. Our qualifications from Lebanon were not recognised in the United Kingdom despite the high grades we received. We certainly wouldn't get into medical school with the qualifications we had. We would have to sit A-level exams, which usually take two years to complete if you are a full-time student. These were non-negotiable. In other words, if we wanted to study medicine in the United Kingdom as home students, we'd have to acquire residency which would mean living for at least three consecutive years prior to starting university and we would have to sit A-level exams and secure straight A grades. And just like that, we learned that instead of entering university as people our age usually do, we had just been set back by three years, the duration it usually takes to complete a bachelor's undergraduate BSc degree or a PhD.

We were in a state of shock when we discovered this. Not so much about having to sit A-levels; a part of us was hoping that the qualifications we had with the high grades we obtained would be enough. It didn't shock me too much that our qualifications and grades wouldn't suffice. It was having to delay going into university for an extra year, not a 'gap year' that many younger people our age would do after completing A-levels during which they would usually go backpacking the world. So, what would we do during this 'extra year'? Well, it didn't look like we had many options. I would continue cleaning floors, stacking shelves and filling fridges for 60 to 70 hours per week on minimum wage.

And that's what I did. I realise that things could have been a lot worse. But seeing people my age going to university and studying medicine (which was my dream) and seemingly having a lot of fun was depressing. Something didn't feel right. Something didn't feel fair. Did I really deserve this? All those sleepless nights burning the midnight oil studying for exams and getting the highest grades so I can get into university and for this not to happen. It was deeply disheartening.

When colleagues at work were feeling more social towards me (not that they were antisocial but it always felt like there was some type of barrier) they'd ask me about what I wanted to do with my life. I'd say I want to become a doctor. I don't ever remember receiving a positive reaction. It felt like they thought I was delusional. Indeed, a few colleagues would say I had no chance. But there were some colleagues who I felt may have resented me. I mean, who do I think I am? Coming to England with these wild ideas that I'll break the poverty cycle and I'll become a doctor and save lives and earn respect from society? No, you'll spend the rest of your life stacking shelves and struggling to make ends meet like the rest of us. How dare you come here with your ambition and your dreams! You fool! Indeed, there was always this pervasive sense that I wouldn't make it. It wasn't just a sense, it felt more threatening than that. It felt like people would sabotage me to prevent me from succeeding.

I remember one morning waking up. It was cold and dark and raining outside. I missed the 5.00 am bus service to the city centre and had to wait for another hour in the pouring rain for the next service. I got to work late and was drenched. I was scolded by my line manager who constantly complained the floors weren't clean enough. I then rushed to my second job and found the fridges were all empty and needed filling. So I spent the entire day going in and out of the refrigerated stock room transferring produce from there to the fridges on the shop floor. I accidentally dropped a milk carton and it burst open on the floor causing a huge mess. The milk splashed on a customer and I apologised profusely, however, they still yelled at me. My line manager had a right go at me afterwards and shouted, 'Clean it up!', which I dutifully did. I ended the day and it was dark, cold and raining outside. While I was waiting for the bus, a car passed by and drove over a puddle (deliberately I think) and I was drenched in water yet again. At that moment I couldn't take it anymore and I started to cry. I then remembered graduation day in Lebanon literally only a couple of months prior. I remember being awarded the plaque for graduating top of my class and the standing ovation I received. I remember basking in the unconditional love that I was immersed in for I was surrounded by my family and friends. I remember how at that moment I felt like anything was possible. I then looked at my situation now, how distant if not far-fetched that dream was, how I couldn't derive comfort from the immediate presence of my loved ones because they were all so very far away and I didn't know any people in the United Kingdom other than my brothers and my best friend, which made me cry even louder and harder. I was only 17. I don't think I had the emotional resilience and maturity to manage and cope with the circumstances that I was in. And I didn't have any support, formal/professional, informal or otherwise.

The following year, after working for approximately 50 to 60 hours per week stacking shelves, cleaning floors and filling fridges, I enrolled into a sixth form college to sit the required A-level exams. If I had learnt anything from the previous year it was that I had to get into university, more specifically medical school, and that 'higher learning' was the path most suited for me. There was a sense of urgency. I would do anything to make it happen. I think I had great hopes that we would make new friends in sixth form. But again, our disappointment was as great as our hopes were high. It wasn't from lack of effort. I really tried my best to integrate. But the cohort of students I had joined had known each other since they were little kids. They had all grown up together. They shared many memories and they had many adventures and misadventures together. The cliques were formed and seemingly impregnable. I think we were just too different from them. They couldn't relate to us and our struggles and hardships.

The teachers were also having difficulty trying to figure us out. Our maths teacher was understandably guarded and didn't know what to make of my extrovert tendencies. It was definitely over the top from me, such was my desire to have authentic connections with anyone. But nonetheless, she was very kind and incredibly supportive. She was an outstanding teacher who loved the topic she taught and she wanted her students to succeed, including us. My form teacher was a godsend. She was compassionate, gentle, sincere and supportive. I remember when I returned to the sixth form for a visit when I was a medical student and she just looked me square in the eyes and bluntly said, 'I don't know how you did it.'

When we were sixth form students we continued to be independent. In other words, we were entirely reliant on the money we earned from work. Again, work wasn't a 'side hustle'. We didn't work because we wanted to save up to go on holiday to Belize or to buy that Louis Vuitton bag. We had to work to earn the money to pay for rent and food. I didn't know any other people in my situation, who had left their family behind in another country and who were working to survive and studying to get into university. I continued to work full-time hours but changed my shift patterns. I would work 14 hours on Saturday and the same on Sunday. I would work 4-hour shifts in the evening on Mondays, Wednesdays and Fridays. I would usually wake up between 4.00 and 5.00 am, and I'd be back home around 11.00 pm or midnight. It was exhausting. Looking back, I would have to agree with my form teacher – I don't know how I did it.

When you are working full-time to survive, this can pose a constant threat to obtaining the necessary grades to get into medical school (straight As in A-levels). I remember being genuinely upset and aggrieved that I couldn't study as much as I worked. It didn't feel fair but there was nothing I could do about it. I didn't want to complain. In fact, I felt extremely fortunate to at least have the chance of getting into medical school, no matter how high the odds stacked against me were. I think what was driving me the most was the fear of not getting into medical school. My fate, to an extent, was in my own hands. The opportunity was mine to lose.

Securing the grades to get into medical school in and of itself was tough enough. Adding the other layers of having to work to survive, not being socially accepted and being far removed from our loved ones made it even tougher. When we joined the sixth form, we had a meeting with the Head. During that meeting she said something I'll never forget. When she asked us what we wanted to study at university we replied medicine. Her reaction was astonishing. She literally laughed in our faces and retorted, 'You can't study medicine, it's too competitive, choose another course.'

I don't know why she said that and where those words came from but it didn't feel like they came from a good place. What was clear to me was that the Head of the Sixth Form was a proud person. I mentioned I was extroverted and outgoing and I had the habit of saying good morning to people as I crossed them in the corridor, including the Head of the Sixth Form. But she never replied. Her head would remain raised and despite my confidence, I would lower my gaze to the floor.

However, one day there was a sudden change in her demeanour. This was no ordinary day; it was the day that the results of the first A-level exams were released. The Head and all the teachers had access to the results before the students did. As I would normally do every morning, I would walk down the corridor and the Head would walk in the opposite direction. However, this morning was diametrically different to other mornings. I sensed that the Head was feeling awkward and when I looked up, her head wasn't aloft as it usually was when passing by me but instead her gaze was fixed on the floor.

I didn't know why at the time but we would soon discover. When we entered the room for our mathematics class, the teacher had a huge smile adorning her face and she said a loud and enthusiastic 'good morning' to us. She seemed excited! This wasn't like her. She was usually a lot milder in manner, even timid. But she just couldn't stop smiling at us! When I finally received the envelope that contained the results of the tests, I saw that I received 100/100 in my maths exam, and straight As in my other exams. I didn't react at first. I mean, I was used to getting 100/100 for the exams I took in schools in Lebanon. It then sunk in and I started to make more sense out of my situation. The Head of the Sixth Form was wrong about us. We did have what it takes to get into medical school, despite having to work full-time hours to survive. When we said we were determined to realise our dream of becoming doctors, we meant it. During a lecture at Harvard Medical School in 2015, a lecturer shared a quote by Thomas Edison: 'Vision without the ability to execute is a hallucination.' But we weren't hallucinating or delusional. We had a vision and the ability to execute, and we had self-belief in spades.

I continued to work full-time over the next two years and throughout this period I was preparing for A-levels. Despite the constant threat that this posed for me to secure the necessary grades to get into medical school, I received straight As. In 2003, I matriculated into Manchester University where I was made an offer to study medicine. My dream was coming true. I was about to start the next chapter in my life. Hopefully this chapter will have fewer obstacles. I mean things couldn't get any tougher and traumatic, could they?

Before moving onto the next chapter, I want to comment on the assumptions people often make about the hardships that a person faces merely based on the labels (e.g., refugee, asylum seeker) that they have been given. Just because a person may not be a refugee or an asylum seeker, it does not mean that they 'had it easy'. It's not a competition as to who had it tougher, and we shouldn't make comparisons. What we need to do is take the time to get to know a person's story with an open mind and an open heart. When we uncover distress (which is subjective by nature) we should never invalidate it. I came across a quote about invalidation which I thought was incredibly powerful: 'Saying to someone they shouldn't be depressed because others have it worse is like saying to someone they shouldn't be happy because others have it better.' Without validation, I think there can be little, if any, healing.

4
Breaking Point

So much happened to me during this chapter of my life, the good, the bad and the ugly but unfortunately mostly the bad and the ugly. Indeed, this period perhaps was the most traumatic and transformative in my life. The adverse events that I was involved in during medical school will provide insights into the structures and scaffoldings in place that permit such callous human rights violations to occur. I must warn you that the content of this chapter is darker. It's heavy and intense reading and can be triggering. But I think it is important and necessary to discuss. Sometimes, we can feel forced to sanitise our stories. However, this wouldn't be an accurate reflection of our realities and those in search of the truth would be denied it if we omitted the negative content.

Manchester as a city, certainly when I first arrived, seemed bigger, better, more diverse and vibrant than Leeds. I moved into student accommodation in Fallowfield, the beating heart and hub of student life in Manchester.

Before starting university, it didn't occur to me that people from low-income backgrounds are under-represented in medical schools to the extent that studying medicine is the preserve of the middle and upper classes. However, medical schools must be a reflection of the diverse communities whom doctors serve. This is why it is necessary to fund broadening participation initiatives to include people in medical schools who come from a range of diverse socioeconomic, gender, race and faith backgrounds – especially people from minority backgrounds.

In my first year of medical school, I thought to myself, 'We are all on a level playing field now, we are all "freshers"', a term used to denote first year university students. No cliques had been formulated just yet. I wouldn't be socially excluded by the other students like I was in Leeds. Here, in medical school, I was surrounded by like-minded and like-hearted people.

I felt I had been shackled for so long and now, after all these years, I was emancipated, and I could finally be my true effervescent self. Being a lot more vocal back then, I attracted far too much attention, positive and negative, and to be entirely honest, I regret this now. Perhaps it was a trauma response after being 'locked up' for so long? I didn't know I was enacting some type of compensatory unconscious defence mechanism. I knew how horrible it felt to be shunned and socially excluded and I wanted to transmit the signal that I would never make you feel the way I was made to feel. In other words, you could always count on me to reciprocate your overtures and say 'hi' every time if you said 'hi' to me first.

In medical school, I was still an independent student and even though I had a student loan (which, at the time amounted to £4000 per year), I knew I needed work to survive. Just around the corner from where I was living in the student accommodation was Subway. I landed a job as a 'food artist'. I don't remember many other students having to work to make ends meet. Most of them appeared to come from wealthy backgrounds. They would go on holidays, party all night long and sleep in during the weekends and not have to worry about how they will finance their lavish lifestyles. Their parents covered all the costs. It was not uncommon for parents to arrange for groceries to be delivered to their doorsteps.

I realised that my background was very different to the backgrounds of most of the students in medical school. During my first year I really struggled with having to work to survive while also having to prepare for high-stake exams. The stress of working was adversely affecting my academic performance. I really struggled with my identity back then too. As a practising Muslim, I would pray five times per day, fast during the holy month of Ramadan and abstain from consuming alcohol or taking any illicit substances. I became less disciplined and devout with my faith, which was an integral ingredient of my identity. This loss profoundly affected my psychological wellbeing. And though I deviated from the path of righteousness, I am grateful that I never resorted to self-medicating or chemical coping. Drinking alcohol and taking drugs are not uncommon among people with mental health problems, especially amongst medical students, and they can be a form of escapism and distraction from the cruelty of their condition and circumstances. However, such relief is temporary. Self-medicating is a maladaptive means of coping that can result in cumulative long-term damage to both mental and physical health.

My first year was tumultuous but I still worked and studied hard, and I was able to pass all my exams. The following year I was a lot more settled. In fact, it was the best year I had in medical school. I worked the entire summer in a Jamaican restaurant and saved up a decent amount of money. I was also offered a spare room to live in for free with fellow medical students, an offer which I accepted with alacrity. It meant I didn't have to work for the first time since arriving in England and I could fully focus on my exams. I felt a lot more stable and my mind was a lot clearer. My academic performance consequently improved considerably and I passed all of my exams comfortably at my first attempt.

I was functioning a lot better socially too. I was starting to understand how some people from a different cultural background might construe my overtures as overfamiliar and intrusive. I felt a lot more confident and secure in myself. I was physically active; I would exercise daily and this definitely contributed to my mental health resilience, although at the time I didn't realise and appreciate that. Lifting weights on a daily basis also helped increase my self-esteem.

I returned to Lebanon after completing my second year to surprise my family and they were overjoyed to see me.

I visited my mum on the farm when she was with my grandparents. She was in the middle of preparing a huge meal but when she saw me she dropped everything, ran towards me and just wouldn't stop kissing me! My dad was also delighted to see me when I paid him a surprise visit in his clinic.

It was in my third year of medical school that there were changes in my mental health. I can say this now with the benefit of hindsight and with the specialist knowledge I have acquired as a consultant psychiatrist. At the time, however, I was not conscious or aware of these changes. I was still, up until that point, within the parameters of functionality. But looking back, I was far too elated and I was having difficulty governing my impulses. My mood would fluctuate and I became more irritable and argumentative when usually I was far better at maintaining my equanimity to the extent it was almost impossible to perturb me. My sleep patterns were also highly irregular. My grades plummeted and my clinical placement supervisors wrote negative reports about me. For example, I missed a bedside teaching session delivered by the consultant during my cardiology placement because I couldn't get out of bed. I had lost all interest and motivation to attend. I woke up late in the afternoon to a text message that had been sent to me by one of the other medical students. She informed me that the consultant, 'Wasn't very impressed that I hadn't shown up that morning for bedside teaching without a valid reason.' I can understand why he had said this. It wasn't because I wasn't bothered, after all, it was my dream to get into medical school. Little did I know back then that a symptom of major depressive disorder is loss of interest in things that were previously joyful. And slowly but surely, the vice of depression continued to compress me.

I am not sure why my mental health gradually deteriorated. I can only surmise that the accumulation of stress, strain and trauma over the years finally caught up with me. I had simply had enough. I was fed up with having to work to survive and watching my peers go on wild spending sprees without a worry or care in the world. I also made many blunders, too many to count and too ashamed to list them here. For example, when my mood was less stable, I was unable to manage my finances. My housemates were finding it increasingly difficult to live with me. I was too chaotic and disorganised for their liking and I understand why they felt that way.

It was only when I had a meeting with the Responsible Dean that I snapped out of whatever spell I was under. He would read the negative reports written about me by my clinical supervisors and comment on my poor grades. He even showed me a chart that predicted my trajectory, which was a downward slope towards failure. I remember interrupting him and saying, 'My approach to medicine this year has been completely wrong.' I think it was not only what I said but also how I said it that prompted him to raise his head (up until that point his head was buried in his notes). He could discern sincerity in my voice and a determination to transform my ways. But he also saw my refusal to externalise and a willingness to accept that I was in the wrong.

Indeed, my approach to medical school and life in general transformed overnight. I started to devour my textbooks. I would study for hours on end and deep into the night. Even whilst I was walking I would be reading my textbooks. I'd even bump into the lamppost whilst engrossed in a medical textbook! I don't know what happened to me and I can't explain it, but my cognitive processes accelerated and my mind became more receptive to medical knowledge. Studying this intensely – up to 14 hours a day – lasted for approximately six months. The amount of knowledge that I acquired during this period was so vast that it covered me for the subsequent years that I was unable to study because of how damaged my mind was from the adverse effects of trauma.

The other students started to notice how hard I was studying and how much medical knowledge I had acquired. The thing about medical school is that the competition between students is fierce. Each student is out for himself or herself or at least so it seems. The ferocity of this competitiveness was to the degree that even close friends wouldn't share questions from previous exams with each other!

The change in my approach to medical school and life didn't go down too well with my housemates. The atmosphere in the house became unbearable to the extent that I could no longer live there. So, I packed my bags and left and knocked on another friend's house late at night and asked him if I could stay there until I could sort my accommodation situation out. My friend kindly obliged.

Around this period there were other stressors that were also accumulating and compounding. But I refused to accept that maybe I needed some help.

On the morning of the clinical exam, I went to the teaching hospital where it was taking place. The cohort was divided into different cycles. Whilst waiting to be called, I and other students who were allocated to Cycle 3 were busy studying from our medical textbooks and notes. Someone then entered the room and called my name. I didn't think anything of it at the time and I dutifully followed her. We entered her office and she asked me to take a seat. She didn't understand why I was waiting with this group as I had originally been allocated to Cycle 2 – who had already taken their exams. It then dawned on me that I must have been so stressed and overburdened that I simply wrote down the wrong cycle. The medical school didn't allow me to join another cycle to take this clinical exam. And there you have it – six months of studying on average for 12 to 14 hours a day and I wasn't able to demonstrate the vast amount of knowledge and skill I had acquired as a result of my own clerical error.

A meeting was then arranged with the Responsible Dean and it was during this meeting that the floodgates opened and there was an unfiltered torrent of words. My thoughts had become so disorganised, my speech so rapid and pressured that I must have sounded incoherent. The dean, immediately recognising the huge distress I was under, advised me not to take a mandatory 4-week

Special Student Component, which was also assessed, but instead to rest and recuperate. And so, on his advice, I did not attend this assessed component of my medical degree, but instead used this opportunity to try to unwind and clear my mind.

The dean was a kind and caring man. To this day I continue to heap praise on him (I can't help it!) Although he is a surgeon, Prof. Ged Byrne is the best psychiatrist I ever met. He provided a safe space for me when I was at my most vulnerable and he never made me feel judged. He's the best listener I've ever met. He didn't listen with the intention of responding, he listened with the intention of understanding. Prof. Byrne was genuinely able to heal me with his listening power. He understood me in ways that I wasn't able to understand myself. He saw the potential and strengths in me that I couldn't see in myself. Most importantly, he believed in me when everyone else had given up hope, including myself. I never felt weak in his presence. I always felt empowered and dignified. He never looked down on me or through a lens that would psycho-pathologize the expression of human emotion. He recognised the distress I was under and the unresolved trauma that was tormenting me. He offered kindness and compassion, not punishment and ridicule. I would go as far as to say that Prof. Byrne's presence in my life is an example of divine intervention, but of course I would say that given my beliefs. Prof. Byrne did everything he could in his power to support me. He genuinely wanted what was best for me. To this day we remain in touch.

My case was referred to the Progress Committee for review. A date was confirmed for the meeting but I was informed via email that I didn't have to attend. At the time, I didn't think much of it. I just thought everyone was on my side and that they would be as understanding and supportive as Prof. Byrne was towards me. It was one of the biggest misjudgments I ever made, the consequences of which would devastate and traumatise me. It pains me now, decades later, to think about it.

All I had to do, I was 'advised', was to send a supporting statement explaining why I didn't show up for the clinical exam and for the 4-week assessed Special Student Component. I can't remember what I had written down in my supporting statement exactly, but I do remember wanting to be as discreet as possible. I had been paying the price for opening up and making myself vulnerable to others and I didn't want to go through that trauma all over again. I don't know what came over me. I thought the Progress Committee would just believe every word I said. And why not? I was telling the truth. 'My concerns and responsibilities were more than the average medical student.' I didn't think that I needed to explain myself further. The people in the medical school who I sent the supporting statement to would email me a few times afterwards asking if I wanted to send any further information. But I responded stating that that wasn't necessary because I genuinely thought that it wasn't. And I thought that was the end of that. So the Progress Committee had their meeting and a few days later they sent me the outcome via email. But just before I opened the email, I turned the TV on and witnessed the IDF bombing my hometown in Lebanon. Expecting that the Progress Committee would be supportive and understanding in their statement, nothing could have prepared me for what I was about to read.

The outcome stated that I had 'left medical school without completing the year'. That opening line hit me like a ton of bricks. I felt a fist in my stomach and an excruciating pain in my chest and I wasn't able to breathe. I would later learn from my psychiatrist that these were the somatic symptoms of a panic attack, which I read about often in our medical textbooks but never realised how severe and debilitating they were. But it didn't stop there. They justified their conclusion by stating I didn't take the clinical exam and that I didn't attend the Special Student Component, which wasn't strictly true. I had prepared thoroughly for the clinical exam but I simply showed up to the wrong cycle because of the tremendous stress I was under, and I didn't attend the Special Student Component on the advice of the Responsible Dean, not because I didn't take my medical studies seriously. It was the final sentence that was the dagger in the heart: 'If you don't send an email response then we will consider that you have left the course.' I couldn't believe the arrogance! After everything I did to get into medical school, I wasn't going to bother sending them an email to stay on the course! That's how little they thought medicine meant to me!

I cannot overstate how devastating this outcome was to my mental health and my life. Looking back, it felt like I was being relentlessly and heartlessly attacked on all fronts: my friends who I used to live with, the medical school, the war in Lebanon. I refused to be a passive victim so I fought back and sent an email to the medical school with my honest thoughts on how they treated me. I can't deny it, I was enraged. How dare they speak to me as if it didn't matter what I said or how I felt or what I thought. As if I didn't matter.

But nothing I said changed anything. The medical school said I had no other option but to repeat the year and because I didn't respond before the deadline, I had to take a year out (a war in Lebanon apparently was not mitigating circumstances for not being able to respond on time). It wasn't only what had been done to me but it was the manner in which it was done that was so damaging and harmful. Just like that, another two years of my life down the drain. What followed was a major depressive episode, the symptoms of which were so severe and debilitating I simply was unable to function. I felt hopeless and worthless. I blamed myself for everything and felt like a complete and utter failure. I was immobilised by the excessive guilt. I didn't have an ounce of motivation to do anything. I couldn't even get out of bed. There was not a trace of pleasure or joy in my life. My mind was obliterated. I couldn't concentrate and I wasn't able to carry a conversation. I remember retreating and isolating myself from everyone.

I was rendered impoverished and homeless and I didn't have a penny to my name. I spent a night sleeping rough on the cold and hard streets of Manchester. I went to the mosque and asked if I could sleep there but they had a 'no sleeping in the mosque' policy. A man who attended the mosque for morning prayer and who I had never met before kindly offered me a place to sleep in his home for the night. Subsequent nights I would 'sofa surf'. I eventually found a room in a squalid and dilapidated terrace house in one of the roughest areas of Manchester. I remember when a friend was looking for a place to stay and he slept over for a few nights. I remember the look of shock on his face. He went as far as to say it was a health hazard. I think he was referring to physical health but it was a hazard to mental health too.

These were the darkest days of my life. It took me years to recover from these devastating and severe symptoms. It was enough to drive any human over the edge. There were times I felt suicidal. Thanks be to God that my Islamic faith deterred me from acting upon these seductive suicidal impulses because ending your own life is 'haram' or forbidden in Islam. My faith was a protective factor against suicidal behaviours and, as shall be discussed later in this book, was a factor that contributed to my mental health recovery and is a factor that contributes to my mental health resilience.

There's a lot more that I can say about the horrendous treatment I received in medical school. I was even psychologically tortured, the details of which I will spare you. I've had enough of reliving it in my mind and ruminating on it. Suffice to say there are structures and scaffoldings in place that permit such torture to happen. When you do have a meeting with 'Student Support' (a misnomer that lulls you into a false sense of security) there's a reason that they don't use audio visual equipment to make a recording of the meeting. There was a person who sat next to the 'Lead' who would be discreet (you wouldn't even notice them) and they would write what was allegedly verbally exchanged. This can and was weaponised against me. Think about it for a moment. Why would they include anything wrong that they did to me in the minutes of the meeting thereby incriminating themselves? Of the many meetings I had with them, the written documentation seldom if ever accurately reflected the reality. If I ever had the courage to report them to a regulatory body it would be my word – a brown Muslim medical student with a mental health condition – against their word – a white consultant psychiatrist affiliated with a powerful university with seemingly unlimited resources at their disposal. I didn't stand a chance. No exaggeration, I have never met a person more manipulative and wicked than the 'Lead' whose name I am afraid to mention because we live in a world that protects the perpetrator and punishes the victim. I think he displayed psychopathic personality traits and that he had a Machiavellian personality structure. The amount of harm this 'doctor' has caused me is immeasurable. What a disgrace and failure that such structures existed in a medical school in the United Kingdom that allowed such horrific abuse to happen.

The struggles with the medical school continued and I was made to repeat another year. Suffice to say it only served to increase my misery further. I refused to attend my graduation ceremony out of protest. Finally, I had power over something and I wanted to convey the message to them that they should be ashamed for what they did to me. I had to go through all that abuse, trauma, suffering and anguish – to hell and back – just to qualify from medical school?! I don't know how on earth I emerged from medical school alive. The person who emerged was definitely not the same person who entered. I was irreversibly damaged. I wish I could say it's behind me, but evidently it's not. Most days I get by. But from time to time the traumatic memories resurface and torment me.

If I have learned anything from the experience, psychological torture can be just as devastating and lethal as physical torture, if not more. I chose to study medicine and become a doctor to help people. It was at this point I began to re-evaluate what branch of medicine I should specialise in. I thought maybe the people who needed the most help were those with mental health problems, victims of psychological abuse and torture? I wondered if I should consider using the insights and personal experiences with mental health struggles to help heal others with mental health struggles? I asked myself: should I forget about becoming a cardiothoracic or plastic surgeon and consider psychiatry as a career instead?

5
Recovery and Discovery

Just because someone is functioning, it doesn't mean that they are not struggling with their mental health. Just because someone is struggling with their mental health, it doesn't mean they can't function. . .

Dr Ahmed Hankir on Twitter/X

From June 2006 to July 2011 I continued to experience the symptoms of my mental health condition; however, they would fluctuate in severity and frequency. This was the period during which the Lebanon war was taking place and the time when I received the outcome letter from the Medical School Progress Committee to finishing medical school. I would say that I was 'recovering' or 'in a state of recovery' but I wouldn't say that I had 'fully recovered' after resuming medical school in 2007 (after being forced to interrupt my studies for a year).

Recovery can be an elusive concept and can mean different things to different people. I think it's reasonable to say that recovery is a subjective phenomenon. I remember during an interview for an academic position at the

University of Toronto, the professor mentioned that there were 'recovery scientists' in the faculty. It was the first time I had come across such a term, and I thought it was amazing. Recovery is a science, but I would argue it is also an art.

Only last month, I was invited to deliver a lecture about innovative interventions to reduce mental-health-related stigma, at the European College of Neuropsychopharmacology (ECNP) conference in Barcelona. I thought it was very progressive of the ECNP to invite a speaker to give a talk about a topic that is not related to psychiatric drugs. I remember when I was going for my morning run and I saw a couple of people with the ECNP lanyards and identity badges and I said whilst jogging past them, 'Who needs psychotropic medications when you can go for a run every morning!' Although I was kidding with them, you can argue that there is at least a little truth in the joke. It was at the conference that I chanced upon a poster that included the 'CHIME framework for personal recovery in mental health'. I had come across this framework before, but I thought what a coincidence for me to stumble upon it here whilst in the middle of writing a chapter about recovery! CHIME is a mnemonic that stands for the following:

- **Connectedness:** peer support, and social groups, relationships, support from others, community.
- **Hope and optimism:** belief in recovery, motivation to change, hope-inspiring relationships, positive thinking and valuing effort, having dreams and aspirations.

- **Identity:** rebuilding positive sense of identity, overcoming stigma.
- **Meaning:** meaning in mental health experience, meaningful life and social roles, meaningful life and social goals.
- **Empowerment:** personal responsibility control over life, focusing on strengths.

The CHIME framework is a cookbook that provides the ingredients for recovery and, though not perfect, I personally find it helpful.

I mentioned previously that my mind had been obliterated due to trauma, psychosocial stressors and the severity of the symptoms of the mental health condition I had been suffering from. As mentioned, I had acquired a vast amount of knowledge and skills during a particularly fertile period for my mind in which I was able to study for 12 to 14 hours per day for approximately six months. It was the medical knowledge that I was able to harvest during this fertile period – and crucially that I was able to retain and was able to use to pass my exams in subsequent years and qualify as a doctor. My mind was simply unable to acquire and retain further medical knowledge during this period of recovering no matter how hard I tried. The inability to concentrate and retain information are a couple of the many cruel cognitive symptoms a person living with a mental health condition can develop.

I would say the point in which I recovered was when I qualified as a doctor. Being released from that hell hole of a medical school and the people who harmed me and starting afresh was a critical factor that contributed to my convalescence. Also, preoccupation in the form of working as a doctor, the dignity that this conferred upon me, the role that being a doctor played in my professional identity, and the sense of purpose being a doctor generated, all empowered me and helped me to recover.

Wanting to do whatever it takes to get rid of the debilitating symptoms in your mind, brain and body can render you vulnerable to certain entities, not least the pharmaceutical industry. It is perhaps superfluous to add that the pharmaceutical industry's aim is to generate as much revenue as possible, that they don't necessarily have your best interests in their hearts, and they don't always achieve their aims through ethical means. Such entities know your vulnerabilities only too well. They also know you might only have one line of defence left and that you just need a gentle push to take psychotropic medications. And that is the perfect timing, certainly for these entities, to introduce the 'chemical imbalance' theory.

The chemical imbalance theory goes something like this: an authority and trustworthy figure like a doctor explains to you (after attending an all-expenses paid conference by pharma that covered the costs for business class travel and accommodation in a luxury 5-star hotel) that you are feeling down and depressed because of an imbalance of chemicals in your brain. In the case of clinical depression, the chemical serotonin is perhaps the one that has received the most attention. To lift your mood and make you feel better again, we must 'restore the balance'. And that was how the mechanism of action of the antidepressant Fluoxetine (also known by the brand name Prozac) was often framed to patients. This is not to say that the doctors who framed the mechanism of action in such a manner were nefarious. This is what many doctors, including myself, were taught in medical schools.

Fluoxetine is from a class of antidepressants known as the Selective Serotonin Reuptake Inhibitors or SSRIs for short. It was framed to patients that these drugs would prevent the reuptake of the chemical serotonin from the 'synaptic cleft', the gap between the two nerve endings, which would subsequently 'restore' the balance of the chemical serotonin. And voila! Your mood would be lifted, you would no longer be depressed, and you would start to feel alive again. Prozac the wonder drug! As far as pharma were concerned and wanted you to know, there was a biological basis and scientific evidence to prove that these SSRI medications worked. If you were on the fence about whether you should take the plunge and pop the pills, this was all the push you needed.

These SSRIs, according to pharma, were safe. They weren't addictive like other psychiatric drugs such as benzodiazepines (more commonly known by their brand names, e.g., Valium, Xanax and Librium). They wouldn't be, for example, associated with the debilitating symptoms of withdrawal if you stopped taking them. The language that was used is revealing in this regard. Instead of saying to patients who developed symptoms after they abruptly stopped taking their medications that they are experiencing 'withdrawal' symptoms, they would be told that they are experiencing 'discontinuation' symptoms. The connotations of the former would be more suggestive of addiction, whereas the connotations of the latter wouldn't. The point pharma was keen to emphasise was that these drugs are not addictive, and they are safe so you shouldn't hesitate to take them!

The chemical imbalance theory, however, had long since been debunked. It was, however, catapulted back into the international media's attention and public consciousness following the recent publication of a review paper in a prestigious scientific journal. The authors of the paper essentially reaffirmed that there was no robust evidence to prove that depressive disorder was caused by a chemical imbalance of serotonin in the brain. This, however, was conflated by some to mean that there was no robust evidence to prove that SSRIs were effective at treating clinical depression. Prominent professors in the mood disorder field were quick to point out that the gold standard for testing if a medication was effective at treating a condition was through randomised controlled trials (RCTs). An RCT is a study design that basically entails the following: participants of a study with depressive illness were randomly allocated to one of two groups: a group that received the antidepressant (i.e., 'the intervention group') and a group that didn't receive the antidepressant (the 'treatment as usual' or 'control' group). Validated scales or instruments would be administered on participants in both arms of the study at baseline (i.e., at the commencement of the trial) and at follow up points in the future (i.e., at three months and six months after the trial commenced). These scales or instruments were validated tools that measured/assessed any changes in mood. The prominent professors would cite the extensive research literature that documented the findings of these RCTs that generated data to indicate that antidepressants such as SSRIs were effective at treating depressive disorder.

It does seem, certainly on social media platforms like X, that there is polarisation in relation to SSRIs and psychiatric drugs more generally: in one camp you have individuals who are in favour of psychiatric drugs like SSRIs (usually comprising psychiatrists but also some patients) and in the other camp you have individuals who are against psychiatric drugs (usually comprising individuals who report they have been damaged by psychiatric drugs – 'the prescribed harm community', psychologists, anti-psychiatrists and critical psychiatrists). A raging online battle usually occurs between the two camps for everyone to observe. It is extremely unfortunate that certain individuals in both camps have resorted to attacking one another through insults and intimidation. I have both witnessed these vitriolic attacks firsthand and been the victim of them. I don't think it is ever necessary to be disrespectful or hostile. I have even seen 'prominent' and 'senior' professors attacking others, which continues to unsettle and baffle me.

I get it. I was prescribed powerful psychiatric drugs, and I found the adverse effects intolerable and unbearable, and I had to stop taking them – with the knowledge of my psychiatrist. Often, it can be a trade-off between the debilitating symptoms of the condition we are trying to treat and the adverse effects of the psychiatric drugs that are prescribed. But to say that psychiatric drugs are ineffective for everyone because they didn't work for me would be untrue at best and criminally negligent at worst. Many patients in my clinical practice report they find the medications for their mental health beneficial. I remember when a prominent psychiatrist also said something similar on social media and she was insulted by another prominent psychiatrist for posting such a remark, and I have witnessed firsthand the improvements in the mental health of my patients after receiving medication. There are also many people online who report that medication was helpful for their mental health.

I'll never forget an individual, Mr X, who I was providing care to in my outpatient clinic. For some reason the prescription that I provided was not accepted by the pharmacist he took it to. I didn't make much progress over the phone when I called the pharmacy, so I took it upon myself to go there personally to resolve the issue. My patient offered to give me a lift there (I was a non-motorist) and I accepted. I remember how focused and determined he was to get to the pharmacy and to collect his medications. Upon my arrival, I spoke with the pharmacist, and we resolved the issue. The medications were brought in a brown bag and Mr X dutifully collected them with a discernible expression of relief on his face.

The patient was immensely grateful for my intervention, and he thanked me profusely. I don't know why it affected me so profoundly to see the patient collect the psychiatric drugs from the chemist. I don't think he was aware of a raging battle taking place between those in favour of psychiatric drugs and those against them. I think the anecdote illustrates that, certainly for this patient, the drugs did work, and he knew they worked for him. Moreover, I could sense that he also knew what would happen to him if he stopped taking drugs or, as is commonly written down on a patient's psychiatric notes, 'Became non-adherent with prescribed psychotropic medications', which is usually heralded by a relapse and involuntary psychiatric admission. Mr X had been functioning highly in the community for years. The last thing he wanted to happen was for him to 'relapse' and be detained onto a psychiatric ward. For Mr X, his psychiatric drugs played a critical role in his relapse prevention plan.

A 'one-size-fits-all' approach to mental health doesn't work. For some people, medication isn't helpful. In fact, it can be harmful. For other people medication is helpful. We need to have a personalised and holistic approach to mental health that takes into consideration what works and what is safe for the individual patient and what their preferences are. This must be grounded on a human rights framework. We need to be clear that psychiatric drugs are powerful, that they can be associated with adverse effects and that they can be harmful and, in the rare event, even lethal. That's why patients who are prescribed powerful psychiatric drugs need careful and constant monitoring by trained professionals, especially at the start of treatment, so if there are complications, we can intervene immediately to mitigate the risk of harm.

Talking about psychiatric drugs can be like navigating a minefield. You must tread extremely carefully otherwise you can detonate a bomb that can cause a huge explosion, the damage from which can be devastating. Nowhere perhaps is this more apparent than on social media. It seems to me that a lot of people who have been harmed by psychiatric drugs or who have developed adverse effects have had their experiences minimised, invalidated or dismissed. Many report that they weren't told about the adverse effects or that they were misinformed (i.e., they were sold the 'chemical imbalance theory'). Worse still, there are people who report they were lied to and/or manipulated. Of course, this must NEVER, EVER happen.

When psychiatric drugs are prescribed there should also be discussions about a de-prescribing strategy whereby after a period of sustained stability there would be a plan in place that is co-produced between provider and receiver of care in which the medications are slowly and gradually reduced under close observation and monitoring with a view to discontinuing the medication altogether. The art and science of de-prescribing is a relatively new branch of psychiatry. More funding must be allocated, and more research must be conducted in this important and seemingly neglected area of psychiatry.

Just because we don't know exactly how a medication works, it doesn't mean that we should not prescribe these medications for our patients. There are many medications that treat physical health conditions that we don't exactly know their mechanism of action for but nonetheless we still prescribe them.

I personally prefer non-pharmacological approaches in the treatment of mental health conditions. Not that I'm against pharmacological approaches. I am a consultant psychiatrist after all. I just think there is so much we can do before getting our prescription pads out. That's not to say that for some people, receiving medication earlier isn't helpful or beneficial for them. Early Intervention Services in the treatment of psychotic disorders have been associated with positive health outcomes.

Lifestyle psychiatry has received renewed attention and interest in recent years. The body of evidence for the mental health benefits that lifestyle changes (i.e., improved diet and nutrition, increased exercise) can bring is growing. Personally, the importance of exercise and staying active for my mental health cannot be overstated. My mental health has remained relatively stable for over 10 years without the need for medication despite the severity of my symptoms when my mental health did worsen. I attribute this stability to daily exercise. My faith and the arts also played important roles towards my mental health recovery and continue to play important roles in my mental health resilience. Social connectedness, with my family, friends and with the online community, also helps to keep me on an even keel (again, refer to the CHIME framework).

When your mental health deteriorates and your symptoms are so severe and debilitating you are no longer able to function you can feel that you will never recover. That is certainly how I thought and felt. It's just always there; the thoughts, feelings and symptoms go with you wherever you go. The symptoms can fluctuate in severity depending on the time, but it doesn't ever really go away completely. It's like a grey cloud over your head; the sun might be shining for everyone else, but for you it's dreary and raining. You desperately want the cloud to disappear, but it won't go away no matter how much you want it to. The symptoms can be all encompassing. You are at the mercy of your mental health condition. It's that sharp thorn in your side that is constantly pricking you.

They say desperate times call for desperate measures. You'll do whatever it takes to get rid of these symptoms that are plaguing your life. And that's when the medication comes in. I was not unique in that I was not too keen on resorting to popping pills. Was it just all in my head? Were my symptoms purely down to awry brain chemistry? It felt like accepting medication would be a concession that it was all down to me and my brain. It wasn't because of what happened to me, all the abuse from the medical school, the injustices perpetrated against me, the trauma, the psychosocial stressors. It was me, my mental health, my reaction to what happened to me and my lack of 'resilience' and nothing else. I think that's why the resistance to take medication can be so fierce. Also, there's a huge stigma, more specifically self-stigma. 'Mental illness happens to others, to weak people. It doesn't happen to me.' Taking medication would be tantamount to conceding that you have a mental illness and that you are weak.

However, when the symptoms are not getting any better but seem to be getting worse, you feel fed up. You urgently need to start functioning and living life again. Enough is enough. So, you surrender to your psychiatrist's or GP's advice, accept the prescription and you make your way to the chemist to collect the drugs.

The threshold for prescribing psychotropic medication (psychiatric drugs) for the treatment of mental health conditions is too low in my opinion. It should be a biopsychosocial model of mental health and mental illness that takes full advantage of psychosocial interventions (i.e., talking therapies, social prescribing, lifestyle interventions) but instead it seems that there is a 'bio-biobio' model. In other words, it feels that many psychiatrists focus almost entirely on biological treatments such as psychiatric drugs and don't consider psychosocial interventions to be that important or helpful. With regard to causation, psychiatry again seemingly focuses on biological causes and genetics.

I eventually conceded to taking medication; however, I was knocked out (sedated) by the adverse effects, which were intolerable and unbearable. Many people with mental health difficulties report that they feel brutalised by psychiatry (due to the adverse effects of psychotropic medication, the power imbalance and the stigma that is rampant in the profession). We must adopt a holistic approach to mental health and mental illness that incorporates the biopsychosocial model and spirituality/religiosity. Medication has an important role, but it is certainly not a panacea. . .

Discovery. . .

> The best people possess a feeling for beauty, the courage to take risks, the discipline to tell the truth, the capacity for sacrifice. Ironically, their virtues make them vulnerable; they are often wounded, sometimes destroyed.
>
> Ernest Hemingway

During medical school, I experienced an identity crisis. I remember asking myself, 'Who am I?' I have previously explained how second-generation immigrants can be prone to developing such identity crises. For example, the values that your parents have that were instilled in them come from the culture in which they were raised (i.e., more conservative). And these values can clash with the values of the culture in which you were raised (i.e., more liberal). When I developed a debilitating episode of psychological distress triggered by the trauma of the 2006 Lebanon War, it compelled me to embark on a soul-searching journey, which helped me to find myself and discover who I was.

Being in a state of vulnerability (which can often be the case if the symptoms of the mental health condition you are living with are severe), can help you to discover who your true friends are. I am reminded of a quote from the film *25th Hour* starring Edward Norton, 'Champagne for my real friends, and real pain for my sham friends!' Living with a mental health condition has helped me to discover who my real friends are. I think it is critical that we know who we can be vulnerable with and trust. Friends can help us a great deal but, depending on the situation they can also cause tremendous harm. Think, for example, of the person you considered a friend who betrayed you after you confided in them and how much it hurt you.

I have said in my teaching sessions to medical students that people can be both a protective factor against developing mental health problems or crises, but they can also be a risk factor. Living with a mental health condition can help you to discover that the quality of your social connections can influence your vulnerability. For example, I am extremely fortunate and blessed to have Wassim in my life, whom I would not only consider a real friend but also one of my best friends. Wassim is the kind of friend whom I can just pick up the phone and call if I experience trauma. Indeed, the informal support that Wassim has given throughout the years, and continues to give has been key for my mental health and resilience. In fact, if it wasn't for Wassim, things could have turned out a lot worse for me. He didn't hang up the phone when I called with a tale of woe, he didn't say he wasn't available, he didn't run away or distance himself during times of distress. I never felt judged by him. I felt I could always, without exception, turn to him. Wassim was always there for me. He never made me feel weak. That is a true friend.

I think about how many psychiatric admissions for patients in a mental health crisis could have been prevented or averted if they had a friend like Wassim. Instead, many if not most patients in a mental health crisis are lonely and socially disconnected, which is utterly heartbreaking. The Surgeon General of the United States, Vivek Hallegere Murthy, in a candid and powerful interview embraced his vulnerability and spoke about his experiences with loneliness and how this adversely affected both his physical and mental health. One of the most important virtues, in my opinion, is making a newcomer feel welcome. No exaggeration, that social acceptance and inclusion can literally be lifesaving.

'Don't treat someone as a priority who only treats you as an option. . .'

When teaching medical students, I would invite them to answer the following question, 'What is a friend?' I remember at an event in Manchester, I put forward, 'A friend is a person you can be vulnerable with' and the audience seemed to agree with me. The audience also seemed to agree with me when I said, 'Not all your friends on Facebook are your true friends' (this was back in the day when I used to have a Facebook account).

There is a powerful quote from author Alan Cohen particularly pertinent to people living with a mental health condition which I think can help guide us when considering who a true friend is: 'Those who love you are not fooled by mistakes you have made or dark images you hold about yourself. They remember your beauty when you feel ugly; your wholeness when you are broken; your innocence when you feel guilty; and your purpose when you are confused.'

So, living with a mental health condition, in a way, can help us to discover who our true friends are. They are not the ones who stigmatise you or who run far away from you after you have become unwell; they are, as Cohen masterfully puts it, the ones who, 'Remember your beauty when you feel ugly; your wholeness when you are broken. . ..' I am not saying that we should be quick to judge who a true friend is. After all, the symptoms of a severe mental health condition can be just as perplexing and frightening to them as they are to you, and it can take time to learn and understand this. People over the years have offered genuine apologies to me for how they reacted and initially treated me when I was unwell.

The point is, living with a mental health condition can help us to discover more about ourselves and the people in our circles (where we stand with them and where they stand with us), what our strengths and limitations are, and how vulnerable and resilient we are, amongst other things. I discovered how beholden we are to the power and mercy of our minds and that I wanted to specialise in psychiatry.

That is what I mean when I say, when looking back with the benefit of hindsight and the wisdom that one acquires through life experiences, 'It wasn't so much of a breakdown, but rather it was more of a breakthrough.' This is a quote that I personally created. Reaching 'breaking point' helped me, amongst other things, 'discover' who my true friends are and what the qualities of a true friend should be and how the people who we associate ourselves with can help to 'elevate' us or bring us crashing down and 'destroy' us. Indeed, to conclude this chapter with another quote that I created, reaching 'breaking point' taught me that we should strive to, 'Be the hand that reaches out and stops someone from falling over the edge, not the hand that pushes them. . ..'

6
Bittersweet

After graduating from medical school in the United Kingdom I entered what is called The Foundation Programme, which usually lasts for two years. During those two years, I completed six clinical placements each four months in duration. Each clinical placement is a medical speciality, for example, plastic surgery, cardiology. The Foundation Programme offers different tracks that applicants can choose from. There are many different tracks, each one of which has a combination of medical specialities. The track that I chose consisted of the following clinical placements/medical specialities: Obstetrics and Gynaecology, Gastroenterology, Vascular Surgery, Acute Medicine, General Practice and Accident and Emergency.

When applying to The Foundation Programme, you are ranked based on the total score you receive on your application form. This score is calculated from points in the following sections: outcome of your exams (divided into quartiles, the higher the test result, the higher the quartile you are in and the more points you score), other degrees and awards, and the points you receive on the clinical vignettes section, which describes a clinical scenario. You are rated based on your written response describing how you would approach each scenario. I understand that The Foundation Programme application process has changed since I applied seemingly a lifetime ago!

Medical graduates (including International Medical Graduates or IMGs, i.e., doctors who graduated from medical schools outside the United Kingdom) can choose where in the United Kingdom they want to complete The Foundation Programme depending on which Unit of Application (UoA) they apply to. Some UoAs are more highly sought after, and therefore more competitive, than others like Central London. To get into the more popular and prestigious UoAs you would need to receive a higher score on your application. I completed The Foundation Programme in the northwest of England, mostly in the Royal Oldham Hospital, which wasn't regarded as part of a prestigious UoA but it wasn't regarded as a poor one either.

Graduates usually select a track that includes a medical speciality that they want to specialise in. For example, if you want to become a consultant psychiatrist, you would usually choose a track that includes a clinical placement in psychiatry. You don't have to do this and it's not necessarily disadvantageous if you don't. For example, I didn't choose a track that included psychiatry as a clinical placement, my rationale being that I wanted to be sure that there were no other branches of medicine that I wanted to specialise in. I wanted to get as much exposure and experience in those specialities to help guide and inform my decision making. Not only this, but the patients we treat in other medical specialities often have comorbid psychiatric disorders. For example, it is not uncommon for patients with heart problems to have mental health problems too. So you would still get some experience assessing and treating patients with mental health problems even if you are working in cardiology and not in psychiatry.

After receiving your first payslip you become disillusioned. Prior to this, you might have been under the impression that you will start raking the money in as a doctor, but that is certainly not the case. In fact I, like many doctors, really struggled financially. You try to limit the damage as best as you can. For example, I lived in hospital accommodation, which was more affordable than renting a room or apartment and it would also eliminate the costs of travel. But even then, I still found it difficult to make ends meet. I had to resort to payday loans to get by.

So it doesn't surprise me that junior doctors, especially 'junior junior doctors' like Foundation Doctors who are fresh out of medical school and who are up to their eyeballs in debt, have been striking for pay restoration. Junior doctors have even posted their payslips on social media to educate the public about how little they are earning. Given the responsibilities that junior doctors have – your lives can literally be in their hands – the long and antisocial hours they work, the years of intense studying and the suffering and struggling they go through to graduate from medical school; I think that we are not fairly remunerated. It does feel that there are certain politicians and segments of the media that vilify junior doctors for resorting to industrial action. I know only too well how much it pains a doctor not to go to work to treat their patients, for I have been there myself. But if striking is the only way to fight injustice and to get our voices heard, then strike is what we will do albeit reluctantly and with a heavy heart.

It is important to remember that doctors are human beings too. We have people who are financially reliant upon us and who we must support. We must also pay for expensive postgraduate exams and membership fees (i.e., to the General Medical Council, which is the professional body that regulates doctors in the United Kingdom and the respective Royal College that the doctor is associated with. For doctors working in psychiatry for example, that would be the Royal College of Psychiatrists). These costs accumulate and are substantial.

I realise that not everyone will be supportive of doctors striking. But I hope I've at least helped to humanise the medical profession by describing some of the challenges that we face and the vulnerabilities we have.

Notwithstanding the financial challenges, my experiences working as a Foundation Doctor were mostly positive. Certainly compared to my experiences in medical school, The Foundation Programme was a dream come true. But the thing about trauma is that you often develop trauma responses. For example, one of the many trauma responses I developed was the fear that I would be harassed and harmed by a senior figure like I was in medical school. However, given there was a senior figure who was bullying and harassing me in The Foundation Programme, my fears were founded. In other words, I wasn't simply just being paranoid, which might suggest the fault was with me and my psychopathological reactions. Rather, my reaction was an appropriate response to reality.

I definitely think my experiences with mental health difficulties made me appreciate working as a doctor even more. My background also helps me to appreciate being a doctor in the United Kingdom. Many doctors working in Lebanon would relish the opportunity to work in the United Kingdom. I also think that my mental health difficulties guided and informed my approach to patient care, especially mental healthcare. I feel my experiences made me more empathetic. I don't think my experiences ever hindered me. By the time I qualified as a doctor I was way beyond the worst of it. One thing is for sure, I definitely couldn't have worked as a doctor whilst I was unwell. In other words, if ever I had another episode similar to the one I had when I was a medical student, I wouldn't be able to work as a doctor. Before we develop an episode of mental illness, we often experience early warning signs and symptoms. These can be detected by the person living with the condition and by loved ones and colleagues at work.

I think there is a fear not only amongst the public but amongst other doctors too that you can't function and work if you have a mental health condition. This isn't true at all, certainly not with me. I think we need to improve our understanding of how mental health can 'behave'. Much in the same way a professional footballer who sustained a physical injury due to occupational stressors on their bodies recover after taking time out, doctors can also recover from psychological injuries due to occupational stressors on their minds after taking time out. In fact, they often become even higher functioning due to learned coping strategies that increase resilience. In 2013, I was fortunate to receive the Royal College of Psychiatrists' (RCPsych) Foundation Doctor of the Year Award. The RCPsych awards mark the highest level of achievement in psychiatry in the United Kingdom. I didn't receive this national award despite my mental health condition, I received the award because of it. I feel my experiences have undoubtedly made me more insightful, more empathetic and more driven. I would even say that my mental health condition, in a way, is a superpower. I appreciate, however, that not everyone agrees.

Patients with mental health problems are better at 'reading you' than we give them credit for. They can often tell what your motives for choosing to study medicine were: Was it for the status? The respect? The money? Or was it genuinely because you wanted to help people? I have never shared in a clinical context with patients that I struggled with my mental health. Not that I'm ashamed or reluctant to do so. But because I do a lot more listening than I do talking in that context. But often it feels I 'get them' and that they 'get me too'. It's a sixth sense vibe. Once, when I was working as a Foundation Doctor on the Obstetrics and Gynaecology ward I was providing care to a patient with bipolar affective disorder. Pregnancy and the postnatal period are highly vulnerable times for people with mental health conditions. This patient often said 'I have bipolar. I have bipolar.' During a ward round one morning, she was walking up and down the corridor and instinctively, we gave each other a high five. I was able to draw on my personal experiences to realise how much she valued authentic connections. But it was also a signal to her that together we will overcome her health condition and that there is no shame or stigma or any distance between us. The smile on her face was priceless.

So yes, people living with mental health conditions, including those of us who have experienced severe mood, anxiety or psychotic symptoms and who have recovered, can and indeed should practise medicine. This is our human right. We shouldn't be stigmatised and discriminated against. The importance of emphasising this cannot be overstated. We must give hope to people living with mental health conditions who experience severe symptoms that they can recover and that they can, if they want to, become doctors. Also, educating the public that people living with a mental health condition with severe symptoms can recover and become a doctor if they choose can help to reduce stigma. I have mentioned that the medical profession must reflect the diverse communities we serve – including people living with mental health conditions that have severe symptoms.

I didn't encounter any mental-health-related stigma from colleagues. I think that was because my condition was not 'visible'. Also, I didn't reveal to them that I experienced mental health difficulties. It was only after completing The Foundation Programme that I revealed my experiences to audiences all over the world. I did have to disclose to my employers that I had mental health problems in the past but to their credit they never held that against me. I had recovered, and there was no evident distress or impairment in my occupational functioning.

I did, however, experience stigmatisation from colleagues about my weight. It is not uncommon for people with mental health struggles to also struggle with their weight. Many are familiar with the term 'comfort eating' and that is exactly what I used to do when I struggled with my mental health. My favourite foods temporarily distracted me from the psychological pain of my condition. I had been highly active most of my life and had an athletic physique; however, I 'let myself go' when I was feeling low and depressed, and I turned to food for comfort. But eating high-calorie meals for a protracted period of time is not without its consequences and I piled on the pounds. Once you've put it on, it becomes very difficult to shed it. One of my fellow doctors said, 'You are the fattest doctor on our programme.' These words were hurtful and certainly not helpful.

Weight gain and 'metabolic syndrome' – a constellation of symptoms including weight gain and poor blood glucose control — are not uncommon adverse effects of many psychotropic drugs. These are risk factors for life-threatening conditions such as heart attacks and strokes. These conditions contribute to the mortality gap of 20 years between people living with severe mental illness and those who don't. The reduced life expectancy in people living with severe mental illness is scandalous to say the least. Many people living with severe mental illness who have gained weight at least in part due to their psychiatric drugs also report they are victims of weight shaming. It can be a major reason why people just stop taking their meds and for their mental health to deteriorate as a result.

Upon completion of The Foundation Programme and acquisition of the 'Foundation Achievement of Competency Document', which was what it used to be called back then, you were now in a position to apply for specialist training. As I mentioned before, I was interested in choosing psychiatry as a career mainly because of my experiences with mental health struggles. I was, and remain, convinced that it was not only a strength but it was an advantage. However, not everyone felt that way. There were some psychiatrists who would advise medical students and junior doctors with mental health struggles not to specialise in psychiatry. Apparently, living with a mental health condition would compromise the quality of mental healthcare a practitioner would provide. I personally thought that was nonsense and that such an assertion was never backed up by evidence. It seemed to me then as it does to me now that the psychiatrist(s) who said this to me and who used this reason and reasons like it were trying to cover up their own prejudice and stigmatising views. It was not surprising when these very same psychiatrists, who represented the minority, said that doctors, including psychiatrists, should not reveal that they had and/or have any mental health issues. Indeed, the resistance I faced from such psychiatrists was fierce, hostile and intimidating. Did they believe I would taint 'their' profession by joining 'their' ranks? I can't say for sure why they held such views towards me and people like me who do decide to be transparent about their mental health.

Thankfully, the centralised panel who interviewed me didn't harbour such negative attitudes towards me. The first interview was to assess and determine if I had what it took to work in clinical psychiatry, that is assessing and treating patients with mental health conditions in hospitals and in community settings. I passed that interview with flying colours. I was also interested in a career in academic psychiatry conducting research on mental-health-related stigma. I therefore applied for the prestigious and competitive National Institute for Health Research (NIHR) Academic Clinical Fellowship in Psychiatry at Manchester University. I had co-authored a few research papers that were published in academic journals and I had also given multiple talks at local, regional, national and international events and conferences. I thought I had a decent chance so I submitted my application. I was delighted to be invited for an interview. I still vividly remember the day of the interview. The panel was firm, but fair. They asked difficult questions, but that was to be expected. I was up against stiff competition and they obviously wanted to recruit the best candidate. There were certain moments when I felt, 'It's in the bag, Ahmed!' When they asked me about my experience in leadership, I answered that I was Captain of the university basketball team despite being 'vertically challenged' and I then vocalised 'it's about heart, not height; soul, not size'. I think I charmed a member of the interview panel because he smiled affectionately and warmly to me when I said this. He knew what determination was when he saw it and he could see it in me.

The Chair of the panel was the most challenging, but not in a negative way. He asked me about my publications, noting they were mostly qualitative, but what about the quantitative stuff? Would I be willing to put the work into that? I remember saying I would but he didn't seem convinced. However, for some reason, my experience working as a janitor came up later during the interview. I think I mentioned my background in the application form and how I felt it made me a better doctor and academic. It was at that point I stopped, called the Chair of the panel out, and respectfully and with the full force of conviction said, 'If I'll get up at 5.00 am to clean floors, I'll get up at 5.00 am to collect data.' I remember saying this with all seriousness and self-belief. The reaction was palpable! I could hear the Chair say, 'yeah!' to himself. I think he enjoyed hearing what I said as much as I enjoyed saying it!

The next day, I received an email from the administrative assistant at Manchester University. She advised me that I was made an offer to be a NIHR Academic Clinical Fellow at Manchester University. It was one of the proudest and happiest moments of my life. Even now, reliving the moment and retrieving the memory makes my eyes well up. It's true, the sweet isn't so sweet without a bit of the bitterness. I remember once having a conversation with a fascinating individual on the 'Pullman' or coach from Sidon to Beirut in Lebanon. This was when I was a medical student and I was having difficulties managing my impulsivity. This charismatic character, however, didn't shun me despite what could have been construed as impertinent behaviour. I suddenly asked him, 'How deep is a man's pain?' And he replied almost instantly, with dignity and grace in his voice, 'As deep as his joy.' I was overjoyed to share with my parents the wonderful news of my imminent appointment: Dr Ahmed Hankir NIHR Academic Clinical Fellow in Psychiatry, The University of Manchester.

My post commenced in August 2013. In November of that year, I attended the RCPsych Awards Ceremony where I received the RCPsych Foundation Doctor of the Year for work I had done the previous year as a Foundation Doctor. I delivered an acceptance speech that I think must have been moving because I was approached afterwards by some of the biggest names in the world of academic psychiatry. We had lively and fun discussions during which we exchanged contact details. We would later resume our discussions first via email then during multiple face-to-face meetings. Both professors were affiliated with some of the most prestigious universities in the world and they both wanted me to join them as an Academic Clinical Fellow. I informed them that I had only recently accepted an ACF at Manchester and that I was extremely happy over there. And it was true, the Manchester experience as an ACF had been amazing.

The professors were very understanding, kind and supportive. I think the allure of the institutions was inescapable and the research and funding opportunities were unrivalled. With their backing and support and with more prestigious national awards, papers and presentations to my name, I took the risk and handed in my resignation in Manchester after one year. Looking back with the benefit of hindsight, I know now that was the wrong decision. Before applying for the ACFs at these universities, I secured a competitive scholarship from the Dubai Harvard Foundation for Medical Research to enrol into Harvard Medical School's Global Clinical Scholars Research Training Program. This was a blended learning programme that essentially developed your research and biostatistics skills. I thought I would enrol in the programme because of the skills I would acquire plus because it's Harvard and I thought that was uber-cool (from cleaning floors as a janitor to graduating from Harvard Medical School, who would have known?!).

I completed the programme over a two-year period whilst working locum shifts in Emergency Medicine (these shifts were readily available, plentiful and easy to pick up). It was during this period that I pioneered my anti-stigma The Wounded Healer programme that

I was delivering and evaluating at events worldwide. I didn't receive any financial support. Initially, before making a name for myself and receiving invitations to deliver The Wounded Healer nationally and internationally, I was using the income I earned working as a locum doctor in Emergency Medicine to pay for travel and accommodation.

The time had come for me to apply for the Academic Clinical Fellowships at these prestigious universities. I was invited for an interview and brought my research portfolios with me, which were heaving with evidence of all the talks and academic papers I had given and published respectively. I thought I was a strong candidate. And why not? I had worked so hard and had what I considered solid outputs. Plus, don't forget, I was approached by these prominent professors at these prestigious universities and advised by them to submit my applications and I had their backing. Nothing could have prepared me for what was about to happen.

In the first interview, not a single member of the panel was a person of colour. I bring this up because I think it is relevant and important. To say that racism doesn't exist in universities is untrue at best and gaslighting at worst. I immediately felt uncomfortable and I felt my race and Muslim name had parts to play in how I was being treated. The panel looked disgusted by me. This disgust was not only discernible in the expressions on their faces, but it was palpable. When I was asked what I wanted to conduct research on and I replied, 'On mental health stigma'. One panel member flippantly and mockingly said, 'Isn't that soft?!' as if to undermine the importance of this research area. The other panel members weren't any better; one laughed at me and my response to her question about medical education. I had a solid track record in having taught at most of the medical schools in the United Kingdom – one of the few if not the only junior doctor to have done so. She turned her head from side to side looking at the other panel members trying to cajole them into joining her so that they could all laugh at me in unison. Thankfully they didn't but I am not convinced it was because they didn't want to belittle me. The other panel member didn't even have the courtesy to look at me throughout the entire interview. I remember emerging from that interview feeling absolutely humiliated and, yes, even violated. But it wasn't just that. The injuries from the interview rendered a deep wound that to this day continues to fester.

Usually when you attend an interview, you hear back from the prospective employer informing you of the outcome. The days turned into weeks and still no response. They didn't have a direct email address. Instead, you had to submit a message through a portal. I didn't receive a response after the first submission so I did this several times. They eventually replied to me. Apparently there were only two candidates who were invited for an interview: me and Dr Y. I happened to bump into Dr Y on my way out of the venue where the interview took place. He recognised me instantly as I had lectured him and his cohort at Cambridge University several years prior when he was a medical student. To add insult to injury, not only did they say they had made the offer to him, but they also added if I wanted a breakdown of my interview score and the reason why I wasn't made the offer I would have to pay a fee. I couldn't believe what I was reading. It's fair enough not to receive an offer if there are stronger candidates, but to humiliate someone in such a manner is shameful.

No job is worth compromising your dignity over. No institution, no matter how 'prestigious', has the right to humiliate employees, prospective or otherwise. Your integrity is non-negotiable. Your value and worth are not determined by biases and prejudices of others. If ever you find yourself in that situation, remember you don't have to stay and put up with that abuse and ignominy. You have the choice to get up and go. And don't forget, you are also interviewing them. Do they have the qualities of an outstanding employer that values and supports their staff? Do you really want to work for an institution that treats people in such a disrespectful and unprofessional way? There's a whole world out there and many institutions, organisations, companies and employers who will see your skill set and who will appreciate and value you and see the strengths in you and who will nurture you to be the best version of yourself that you can be and who are desperate to recruit you. Don't you ever forget that. It can take time, and your patience will be tested to the degree you can start losing all hope. But then, these opportunities come knocking on our doors when we least expect them.

Working in Emergency Medicine for the most part was enjoyable. It was, however, very busy! The department was almost always packed with patients. There were occasions at the end of a shift when I thought to myself, 'How on earth did we see all those patients?!' Of course, not every patient who attended Accident and Emergency (A&E) needed limb- or life-saving treatment. A lot of the conditions they presented with could have been more appropriately treated by a general practitioner (GP). But it's human nature to want things done sooner rather than later, especially when it comes to our health. It sometimes felt like we were the victims of our own success in a way. The NHS was until recently considered the best healthcare system in the world. The founding tenet of the NHS is that all people, irrespective of socioeconomic background, should have easy-to-access, high-quality, round-the-clock healthcare that is 'free at the point of delivery', that is, universal healthcare. This is a fantasy in many parts of the world especially low- and middle-income countries like Lebanon where people are dying of treatable conditions simply because they can't afford to pay for healthcare. But you don't have to go to a developing nation to witness the lethal effects of poverty and living in a land where there is no universal health coverage. Go to the United States and you will meet many people with heartbreaking stories to tell about losing their homes and life savings to pay for treatment or worse still dying as a result of not having the financial means to pay for emergency and/or life-saving healthcare. I think when you've lived in a country where healthcare isn't universal, it helps you to appreciate how fortunate we are to have the NHS in the United Kingdom and that we should never take it for granted. That's why when I hear people complaining, relatives of patients vocalising their discontent about their loved ones having to wait in a bed in A&E until a bed on the medical or surgical ward becomes available, it's challenging to hear. Yes, the NHS isn't perfect. Yes, waiting times can seem too long, especially for certain tests like a formal assessment for Autism Spectrum Condition, but at least we have such a precious provision and that is something I am immensely grateful for.

I must give credit when credit is due. Although I worked in emergency departments up and down the United Kingdom, I worked most of my shifts at the two teaching hospitals in Leeds: Leeds General Infirmary (LGI) and St James's University Hospital (known colloquially and affectionately as Jimmy's). The teams in the emergency departments, especially the consultants, were amazing. They were so hard-working, friendly and kind. There was a very positive culture that made you feel supported and valued. I have very fond memories of working in the emergency departments in Leeds Teaching Hospitals and that, along with daily exercise, prayer and performing, definitely contributed to my mental health resilience.

When you work in an emergency department in the late hours of the night providing care to patients who often are the most vulnerable people in society, you see things that not many people get to see. You can see the fault lines where people have fallen through the cracks through no error of their own. Older people who have developed hypothermia and malnutrition because they can't afford to feed themselves or pay to heat their council homes during the winter. A younger woman trapped in an abusive relationship who frequently attends the emergency department with physical injuries as a result of being the victim of intimate partner violence. A girl who cuts herself as a way of coping with traumatic flashbacks of when she was sexually abused by a family member when she was a child.

There were many patients who attended the emergency department after attempting suicide. The two most striking memories were of a patient who was transported to the hospital by a helicopter. He was taken to Resus (the part of the A&E department where the sickest patients with life-threatening conditions are treated) because all the bones in his lower body (including many of his vertebrae) were shattered after jumping off a bridge onto the motorway. This was not his first suicide attempt; apparently, he had jumped from heights many times before. But there was no question that this would be the last time he jumped from a height. The injuries were just too extensive and the spinal cord had been severed by the fractured vertebrae. What type of pain must a person be in for him to be compelled to carry out such an act? I remember how his neck was in a collar and he was unable to move his head. I remember the look in his eyes as he would stare vacantly at the ceiling. I thought about how cruel the symptoms of mental illness can be and how the government has failed to protect him and vulnerable patients like him living with severe mental illness.

The other patient was a man of colour. This was also a suicide attempt. This patient was brought to A&E by

Yorkshire Ambulance Services after a loved one found him with a rope around his neck attached to a banister from which he was suspended in his home. He lay there motionless and, to me at least, he looked lifeless. He wasn't my patient so he wasn't under my care. I had entered Resus to run an urgent test on a blood sample and that's when I noticed him. You could see the scar from where the ligature had been. It was a chilling scene. Whatever compelled him to attempt suicide, he was determined to carry it out. I think about what his circumstances must have been. What happened to him for him to want to end that which is most precious? Did his loved one walk out on him? Was he the victim of bullying and harassment at the workplace? Was he the subject of ridicule and racism? Was he isolated and cut off from society? Did he suffer from a mental health condition the symptoms of which wouldn't stop tormenting him? I remember he was so young. He looked about 17 or 18. About the same age I was when I arrived in the United Kingdom from Lebanon.

I am amongst the extremely fortunate people to have overcome the debilitating symptoms of a mental health condition. Tragically, there are far too many people who don't survive. That doesn't mean that their battle against the symptoms of their condition and the stressful circumstances they were in was any less valiant. Far from it. When people say they were 'lucky to survive' I understand what they mean. It can seem that it comes down to a roll of the dice or chance. It can feel like we are playing Russian roulette given how high the stakes are. Due to my religious beliefs, I would say that it's a miracle that I survived. There are some stressors I know for a fact that are enough to push me over the edge when I am at my most vulnerable. Somehow, whenever I was subjected to those stressors, it would be during a period in my life when I was more resilient; I may have had someone I could have turned to for support (which isn't always the case), or I may have been exercising more and that would have helped to buffer the traumatic effects of stress. Whether you believe it is a matter of chance or not, each and every suicide is a devastating loss and we should never make any judgements about the person who died in such a tragic manner.

7
The Wounded Healer

This chapter is intense and does cover suicidality, so please prime your hearts and minds and brace yourselves, and by all means skip it if you feel you are not emotionally equipped to read it at this moment.

Trauma can be so overwhelming that your thoughts can become scattered. To be honest, it has been difficult trying to organise my thoughts and feelings after my mind was torn asunder by traumatic events. I, however, gave it my best shot and tried in earnest to be as coherent as possible.

According to scripture, 'Persecution – the denial of freedom – is worse than death – the denial of life. . ..' Might that help explain why people who are tormented by paranoid and persecutory delusions are often driven to end their lives? Being a prisoner of your own mind can be an unbearable situation to be in. There are, however, other types of captivity that are equally if not more unbearable. Being in medical school, in a way, can be a form of captivity. It sounds extreme and dramatic I know, but please bear with me whilst I try to elaborate and explain.

As a medical student it is your dream to become a doctor. For you to realise that dream, you need a medical degree. The university has the power to confer that degree upon you. It also has the power to deny you that degree. So, the nature of the dialectic can be framed in the following way: you, the medical student, basically want something (the medical degree) from them, the university. That places you in a position of vulnerability that they can easily exploit.

If you've been labelled a troublemaker, any form of protest to unjust treatment and/or non-conformity is considered deviant behaviour and is used to legitimise punitive measures against you. In other words, they can do whatever they want to you and you can do nothing about it. You have no other option but to put up with the abuse until you are no longer under their power, that is, until you qualify, which can literally take years. You are afraid to blow the whistle or lift your head above the proverbial parapet because we all know what happens to whistleblowers. That was certainly the case with me.

As soon as you graduate from medical school, you leave one machine and enter another. But that's a different beast altogether. You can choose to rage against the former machine now that the restraints and restrictions have been lifted somewhat and the shackles have been removed.

Metacognition has been defined as 'thinking about how you think'. How did I end up thinking like this? I'm aware the language I'm using is loaded and layered. But that's what happens to you after you've been 'held captive' for so long. You feel unable to express yourself due to the fear of the draconian consequences and what will happen to you. You are terrified that they would sabotage you, abuse you, deprive you of a medical degree, shatter your dreams and, in my case, psychologically torture you.

'To be silent is to help the oppressor' says Albert Camus. Even though we serve as a witness of the crimes committed against us, when we are victims of brutal acts, we can feel intimidated into silence. I think the explanation for this is simple enough and involves basic conditioning: the perpetrator has afflicted an enormous amount of pain on us and caused immense suffering and distress. He committed these abhorrent acts unflinchingly, swiftly and without restraint. You live in fear that he would deliver yet another crippling blow. You somehow, miraculously, survived the first one but you don't have the capacity to survive another.

Moreover, the attack was so ruthless and heartless, you are still in a state of shock. You are shocked how someone, no less a person who supposedly is a member of the 'healing and helping profession' and who calls himself a doctor could do something that was so devastatingly harmful. This is the same person who made that most solemn and inviolable of oaths to 'do no harm' (i.e., the

Hippocratic Oath that all doctors must take and pledge allegiance to). I think the reverberations of the shock and trauma stun you into a state of silence and torpor whilst you somehow try to process the enormity of what just happened to you.

Astonishing, then, how he can masquerade as if he is an august individual. A person who has transcended the impulse to retaliate no matter how powerful the provocations. An individual who, unlike the rest of us, occupies and operates on an enlightened plane. It is no exaggeration to state that this is the aura that emanates from him and that, like other people with a Machiavellian personality structure, he is a master manipulator. What a charade!

After I was forced to interrupt medical school in 2006 following the Lebanon War, I would avoid people and isolate myself in the room I was renting in a dilapidated and squalid terrace house in Moss Side. I was confused and lost in the vortices of my own mind. It seemed like all the tears had dried up after the episode of inconsolable crying when the 'insight switch' turned on and I regarded all the damage – seemingly beyond repair – that I had caused whilst in a 'frenzied state of mind'. But that all changed when I managed to scrape some money together to watch a film, *Pan's Labyrinth*, in the cinema. There was something about the protagonist, the innocence of the girl and the purity of her soul that touched me deeply. The storyline was so moving, the floodgates abruptly opened, and all the pent-up pain was unleashed in a torrent of tears. For the first time in a long while,

I felt alive, and it was the power of film that made me feel that way.

Shortly afterwards, I noticed that there was an invitation to perform at a health humanities event at the International Anthony Burgess Foundation in Manchester. I responded to the invitation and found myself on a stage in front of a small audience. I did not have a script and I was not really prepared. I just 'performed'. I started reenacting scenes from famous films and reciting poetry from words that were inscribed in my heart, mind and soul. I received a standing ovation, and I lost count how many people approached me afterwards. That is when I realised how we could harness the power of the performing arts to entertain and engage people and once engaged, we could educate them about mental health and mental illness.

I would have to wait for a couple of years before I returned to the stage. Not because I didn't want to, but opportunities back then seemed to be few and far between. I was unknown back then and I was not receiving invitations to give talks, locally or regionally, and certainly not nationally or internationally. I had to wait patiently for my time to come. When my time did come, I had recovered and qualified from medical school. It was the 2013 Biennial International Conference on Mental Health at Cambridge University. The abstract for my talk entitled, 'The Wounded Healer' was accepted for oral presentation. It focused on my mission of challenging mental health-related stigma. But how was I going to accomplish my mission? I really wanted to be true to myself and to reveal how effective the performing arts can be at healing psychological wounds. It worked wonders for me, so why not for other people? I always felt compelled to share my story and to recite poetry and to re-enact scenes from my favourite films. I found this deeply empowering, therapeutic and cathartic. So, The Wounded Healer was a natural extension of that desire. It was in my heart, mind, body and soul; I just had to emancipate and express myself. I punctuated the performance with facts about mental health and mental illness.

Not only did I receive a standing ovation, but I also received the First Prize in the Oral Presentation Competition. The seed had been planted; I knew what I had to do. I took three years out of my psychiatric training to deliver The Wounded Healer to over 150,000 people in 22 countries in five continents worldwide. Columbia was one of my favourite countries where I delivered The Wounded Healer. It was in a hospital in a remote village in the Andes called Tamesis. The weather was tropical, the people were so warm and welcoming, the coffee was delicious, and The Wounded Healer in Spanish is, 'El Sanador Herido', which I thought sounded a lot like 'matador' and I thought that was pretty cool! Each medical school in the United Kingdom has a psychiatry society or 'PsychSoc'. Since I wasn't really known back then, I had to reach out to every PsychSoc in the United Kingdom. I explained that The Wounded Healer aims to challenge the stigma attached to mental health problems in medical students, break down the barriers to mental healthcare, and encourage help-seeking. The responses

I would get were overwhelmingly positive, however, the PsychSocs usually had a limited budget, so I had to cover transportation and accommodation, certainly at the early stages.

I was inspired to conceive The Wounded Healer because I believed that the mental health of medical students is not spoken about as often as it should be and most (if not all) the talks that were given on this topic were soporific. My argument was, and remains, that to educate an audience you must first be able to engage them. The Wounded Healer is a highly theatrical intervention that disrupts conventional educational approaches and seldom elicits indifference. In The Wounded Healer, I re-enact scenes from famous films and recite poetry to engage audiences and, once engaged, I educate them with the facts. If Jules from *Pulp Fiction* does not galvanise audiences, I do not know what will! For me, delivering The Wounded Healer is empowering and it continues to contribute to my resilience.

The Wounded Healer has been integrated into the medical school curricula of four UK universities. We also secured funding from the Institute of Inner Vision and commissioned The Wounded Healer documentary with filmmakers at the London School of Communication. The Wounded Healer documentary has been screened at film festivals and international conferences worldwide (including the World Psychiatric Association World Congress in Berlin). The Wounded Healer has 'evolved' (as mental-health-related stigma evolves so, too, must our approach to combat it) over the years as I have acquired more specialist knowledge but in essence the substance and core messages remain the same.

The Wounded Healer is an innovative method of teaching that blends the power of the performing arts with psychiatry. The main aims of The Wounded Healer are to engage, entertain, debunk the many myths about people living with mental health conditions, break down the barriers to care and challenge mental-health-related stigma. The Wounded Healer also harnesses the power of storytelling; it traces my recovery journey from homeless and impoverished 'service-user' to receiving the 2013 RCPsych Foundation Doctor of the Year Award and, later, the 2018 RCPsych Core Psychiatric Trainee of the Year Award (the RCPsych Awards mark the highest level of achievement in psychiatry in the United Kingdom – not bad for a 'madman'!). In recognition of my services to public engagement and education, I was a Finalist of the 2015 and 2017 RCPsych Communicator of the Year Award.

One of the many great things about social-media platforms is that they enable you to connect with like-minded and like-hearted individuals all over the world who you otherwise would never have known even existed. Such social-media platforms are of course not without their pitfalls. You can tell who the like-minded and like-hearted people are when you start noticing them 'liking' most if not all your content. You then start doing the same with their content, and before you know it you are both following each other.

Dr Michelle Funk at the WHO was that like-minded and like-hearted person who I connected with on Twitter (now X). I think the reason we gravitated towards each other is that we have a mutual love for a human rights and a humanising approach to mental health.

Not long afterwards, I sent Michelle a message thanking her for connecting, for the content she was posting and for the incredible and inspirational work she was doing with the WHO on the human rights of people living with mental health conditions and psychosocial disabilities. Michelle responded and I felt that was the start of a blossoming and what I hope is a lasting friendship. Recognising that our values and our approach to mental health aligned, Michelle said that she would be in touch with me about collaboration opportunities. I, of course, responded and said I'd be delighted and honoured to work with her in any capacity she felt would be helpful.

A few Zoom calls later and before I knew it, I was catapulted onto the global stage albeit it was a digital global stage since the world was still reeling from the devastating effects of the pandemic. Michelle and her dedicated team at WHO had been working tirelessly on developing an alternative approach to mental health within a human rights framework that was co-designed, co-developed and that would be co-delivered with people living with mental health conditions. This approach was called WHO QualityRights, which is now being implemented worldwide. What disturbed and perturbed

Michelle the most and indeed anyone who has a regard for the sanctity of the human rights of people living with mental health conditions was coercive practice in psychiatry. That is, when patients are admitted into hospital involuntarily and when they are forced to receive treatment against their will. Multiple studies have since been conducted on QualityRights showing how it has been positively received by both providers of mental healthcare and beneficiaries of that care. The data also indicates that WHO QualityRights has reduced coercive practice.

For the global launching of WHO QualityRights e-training, Michelle invited a stellar line-up of speakers including WHO Director General, Dr Tedros Adhanom Ghebreyesus and Lady Gaga's mother, Cynthia Germanotta. As far as Michelle was concerned, notwithstanding the influence that Dr Tedros and Lady Gaga's mother had, the event simply could not, would not go ahead unless someone living with a mental health condition – the very people QualityRights were designed and developed to serve – was also invited to speak at the event. Michelle kindly extended that invitation to me and I duly accepted.

The event was a resounding success and was attended by thousands of people online from all over the world. There were people from diverse backgrounds including and, most importantly, people with mental health conditions, policymakers, psychiatrists, psychologists, social workers, people working in humanitarian settings and non-governmental organisations (NGOs).

Mrs Germanotta kickstarted proceedings by talking about the mental health organisation she co-founded with her daughter, the Born This Way Foundation. She was dignified and spoke passionately and eloquently about the support that her foundation provides and what their aims, values and vision are. I have to say she was very compelling and resembled her daughter a great deal!

It was then Dr Tedros's turn to speak. You could instantly recognise him. During the pandemic it seemed there wasn't a media outlet station that didn't interview him! His was the voice of reason during a tumultuous time in modern human history and despite the global turbulence that Covid-19 caused, Dr Tedros was able to steady the ship and steer us into safety with his leadership, guided by science and humanity.

It was the first time I had ever seen Dr Tedros give a talk at an event I was present in, virtual or otherwise. The first qualities I noticed about Dr Tedros were how kind, gentle, measured and considerate he was. Dr Tedros spoke softly but you could still feel the positive impact of every single word he uttered. He had a calming presence as if nothing in the world could unsettle him. He spoke with conviction and earnestness about the utmost importance of upholding and promoting the human rights of people living with mental health conditions and psychosocial disabilities. He praised Michelle and her team for the painstaking work they carried out to bring QualityRights to fruition and he unreservedly offered them his unwavering support and endorsed their vision.

It was the perfect speech that bolstered morale and inspired us to continue with our mission. When his speech ended, I expected him to leave, not because he was not interested in attending the rest of the event or hearing me speak, but because I just thought here's a person with the weight of the world on his shoulders and a relentless schedule including high-level meetings with global leaders. I didn't think he had time for me. But he made time to attend the entire event and hear all of us give our respective talks. That's the type of person Dr Tedros is. Giving, selfless, sincere, compassionate. And when I saw that he was still there when it was time for me to give my talk, I felt a crescendo of inspiration course through my being.

The content of my talk, which I had prepared and revised extensively prior to the event, remained the same. It wasn't so much what I said but how I said it that was different from previous renditions. I remember genuinely feeling 'elevated' by Dr Tedros's speech and presence. I felt extremely fortunate and blessed. In the Orient, we say what comes from the lips reaches the ears and what comes from the heart, reaches the heart and the words just kept flowing incessantly from my heart.

Dr Tedros then looked up after he was sorting some notes out and our eyes locked. I don't know how else to describe it but at that moment, brief though it was, our souls clicked. I felt it was as if he understood all the adversity and trauma that I had encountered and overcome and I felt the exact same energy emanating from him (Dr Tedros, after all, was a child of war and had endured much trauma and adversity himself). As much as I wanted that moment and feeling to last longer, we were under a strict schedule and I brought my speech to an end.

I remember smiling to myself when the event finished. I was in my apartment in southeast London all by myself. I had just connected on what felt like a deep and authentic level with Dr Tedros, the Director General of the WHO. And it was the most empowering feeling. It didn't stop there though. Soon afterwards, I noticed that I had a new follower on Twitter/X, none other than Dr Tedros himself! I obviously followed him back instantly. Dr Tedros noticed a post in relation to how proud I was to have spoken at the event and to have shared a platform with him. To my amazement he had responded and said that he was proud of me! Being the emotional type, my eyes started to well up. It was one of the best days of my life.

A couple of days later I received a WhatsApp message from Michelle. It seemed like she was desperate to talk to me about something. Whatever it was, it must have been important because she sent an invitation for a formal Zoom meeting.

Michelle wasn't the only person to be on the Zoom call. Gaby, Director of Communications at WHO, also joined us. I would later forge a firm friendship with Gaby. It was impossible not to. We had so much in common. We loved to stay active, we were both big fans of cafe culture but most importantly we both had extrovert tendencies and enjoyed mingling and mixing with other people. I remember when we started the video call, Michelle just wouldn't stop smiling! Her face was beaming with joy! Her energy was so positive.

The WHO World Health Assembly in Geneva was fast approaching. World leaders and health ministers would flock to Geneva to attend and to speak. Every year, Dr Tedros would select a handful of people to receive the WHO Director General Award for Global Health. For the 2022 Award, Dr Tedros selected six individuals and groups of which I was one. Michelle would later say she couldn't believe it when she was told. Not that she didn't have faith in me. On the contrary, Michelle always believed in me and could see the strengths in me that I couldn't see in myself. She was surprised because Dr Tedros has vast and extensive networks that span all four corners of the globe. There were long lists of incredible people from which he could have selected. But he didn't choose them, he chose me. It came at the perfect time; it was during a traumatic period in my life and the belief I had in myself had taken a huge knock. The naysayers had been particularly savage towards me online and that coupled with other stressors were starting to get to me. I'm only human after all.

Being selected to receive this award restored my self-belief. It would also give me the strength to defy and silence the haters. I often say, 'Haters will hate, lovers will love, love will prevail. . ..' I think this was the perfect example of how love did prevail. The love for humanity. The love for kindness and respect. The love for righteousness and decency. The love for service and charity. The love for embracing vulnerability. The love for having authentic connections with others. For me, receiving this award from Dr Tedros were all these things and more.

People often ask me where do we even begin when we want to reduce stigma given that it is seemingly ubiquitous? I respond by saying a good place to start is by being introspective and brutally honest with ourselves to remove any stigma that we might be harbouring. I then add we must provide a platform to people living with stigmatised attributes like mental health conditions and amplify their voices. We must harness the power of storytelling to decrease stigma, debunk myths and break down the barriers to mental healthcare services. Through Dr Tedros's leadership and by him selecting me to receive the award at the WHO World Health Assembly, I was invited on one of the grandest stages I have ever been on.

I remember every detail of that day: when Dr Tedros invited me to join him on the stage; when he looked me in the eyes and said it was a pleasure and privilege to meet me in person; when I was so overwhelmed with emotion as I could see my life playing out before my very eyes, all the trauma, adversity, abuse, stigmatisation, discrimination, racism and setbacks. When Dr Tedros put his arm around my shoulder recognising how I was feeling and what was happening to me his arm was like a soothing balm. We embraced each other on the stage in front of the audience, in front of the world.

I remember in my acceptance speech paying tribute to my father, Dr Zakaria Ahmed Hankir, Hakeem Shaab 'the people's doctor' who doesn't charge the poor, including many Palestinian and Syrian refugees who he treats in his clinic in Sidon, South Lebanon. I remember receiving a standing ovation at that point, the only speaker at the high-level meeting to have received that honour.

The international media, including the national media in Lebanon, had also captured the event. Back home in Lebanon, my winning the Award was apparently quite a big deal. I was told that I was all over the news. The health minister of Lebanon attended the WHO World Health Assembly, and he didn't waste any time sharing the story of my success. I was getting phone calls from political leaders who thanked me. They said I had brought great pride and honour to Lebanon, a small country on the Mediterranean coast in the Middle East.

The country had been ravaged by years of economic mismanagement, political corruption and social unrest. The pandemic had brought the country to her knees. But it was the blast in the port of Beirut, reportedly the largest non-nuclear explosion in modern history, that really traumatised the people of Lebanon. They desperately needed some good news, a positive story of hope and recovery that would restore a sense of national pride in a country that was once brimming with it but had lost most if not almost all of it when the plug was pulled by the blast, and it had all been drained away.

It was overwhelming if not unfounded to be branded 'a national hero' by the media and a symbol of defiance, resolve and resilience. If, however, by disseminating my story we could spread hope then I was fully in favour of my story being shared to whoever wanted or even needed to hear it.

Receiving the WHO Director General Award in Geneva was, and remains, the happiest and proudest moment of my entire life. The memories will remain deeply embedded in my heart of hearts for years and years to come.

I hope my story is further evidence that people living with mental health problems can, with the right support, recover, function, and even realise their dreams. Because if I can recover and realise my dreams, other people out there with mental health difficulties can do it too.

Just when I thought that was enough glory to last a lifetime, I was fortunate and blessed to receive another prestigious award a few months later! In November 2022, I received *The Sun*'s Who Cares Wins Caroline Flack Mental Health Hero Award for my contributions to helping prevent suicide. The Wounded Healer aims to challenge toxic masculinity, which is a factor that contributes to suicide amongst men, certainly in my opinion. Caroline Flack was a British television personality who was adored and admired by many. Caroline tragically died by suicide and the mental health hero award was set up in her honour.

In my Wounded Healer talk, I explain how perpetuating the negative stereotype that men who express their emotions (especially men who cry) are weak contributes to toxic masculinity, which permeates in some regions and communities more than it does in others, for example, the Middle East and North African (MENA) region. This toxic masculinity, in my view, is contributing to the male to female suicide ratio of 3:1. 'Release the pressure valve', 'Don't keep your feelings bottled up', 'Express your emotions', 'Let it all out . . .', are the slogans of suicide-prevention campaigns targeting men. However, when the former heavyweight champion of the world Anthony Joshua was unable to reclaim his championship belts from Oleksandr Usyk after battling him in another bout in Saudi Arabia, he was heavily criticised for expressing his emotions. Not by Usyk – if anything the Ukrainian was incredibly understanding and empathetic towards his adversary – but by segments of the mainstream media.

The star-studded awards ceremony was attended by celebrities including the former heavyweight champion of the world Anthony Joshua and politicians including the Prime Minister Rishi Sunak and King Charles III himself. Glamorous English television personality Davina McCall presented the awards. I will never forget how kind, caring, gentle and sincere Davina was towards me. Despite her fame, she was so down to earth and humble and she comforted me and instantly made me feel at ease. Davina was also looking very elegant, fit and stunning as she usually does! I started my acceptance speech by reciting the lyrics of 'I heard it through the grapevine' by Marvin Gaye. Something to the effect, 'I know Marvin Gaye said a man isn't supposed to cry, but I respectfully disagree. We need to rewrite the narrative on what it means to be a strong man.' I think my words resonated deeply with the audience and Anthony Joshua particularly, because I received a rapturous round of applause after uttering them. It was at that moment – when I noticed Anthony Joshua was clapping for me – I confessed my love to him! 'I love you AJ!'

After the award was presented to me (and I had received a personal message from Formula One superstar Sir Lewis Hamilton congratulating me!), I returned to my table. However, someone then suddenly grabbed me by the arm, and I was taken to AJ's table where Mel B (more popularly known as Scary Spice) was sitting next to him. Mel B was very dignified and gracious, and I was touched by her gesture when she gave up her seat for me to sit next to the former heavyweight champion of the world so we could 'talk on a level'. There is a beautiful picture online of me holding AJ's hand and my arm wrapped around his neck and both of us smiling at each other.

When I spoke with AJ 'on a level' I revealed to him that I had prayed to God whilst I was in the venue where the event took place just before the ceremony started. AJ, the former heavyweight champion of the world, said that I humbled him and invited me to train with him in his gym. It was another unforgettable moment in my life. The Wounded Healer had played such an important role in helping to create this moment.

I hope that my acceptance speech at *The Sun*'s Who Cares Wins Awards – that was captured on national television – helped to rewrite the narrative on what it means to be a strong person and that my core messages of expressing our emotions irrespective of our gender identity and seeking help are signs of strength, not weakness. Will that help to prevent suicide, especially amongst men? I certainly hope it does. Remember lads, letting it all out, expressing our emotions and crying doesn't make us any less of a man. So, don't keep all the pain bottled up, but instead release that pressure valve.

I will finish by quoting UFC fighter Paddy Pimblett in relation to when he discovered that a friend of his had tragically died by suicide. In an interview following a bout that he had won, Paddy emotionally exclaimed, 'I know I'd rather my mate cry on my shoulder than go to his funeral next week . . . Let's get rid of this stigma and men start talking.'

8

Canaries in a Coal Mine

I am not an expert or '*alem*' in the Islamic sciences by any stretch of the imagination. I have some Islamic knowledge that I have acquired over the years through independent study but I have never received a formal education. I certainly do not have an '*ijazah*' or licence authorising me to transmit Islamic knowledge issued by someone who already possesses such authority. That being said, the prophet Muhammed (PBUH) did say in a hadith: 'Convey from me, even if it is a single verse . . . .' In other words, not being a scholar in Islamic sciences and/or not being in possession of an *ijazah* shouldn't stop or deter the dissemination of Islamic knowledge. However, it is critical that the person who spreads that knowledge is certain that it is authentic and obtained from a reliable and reputable source so as to prevent the spread of misinformation and/or disinformation, which could result in a lot more harm than good.

Islam is a monotheistic religion, which teaches that there is one God who created Heaven and Earth and everything in between. Islam has five pillars:

1. The shahadah or declaration, 'I bear witness that there is no deity worthy of worship save Allah (God) and I bear witness that Muhammad (peace be upon him) is the messenger and the final prophet of Allah.'
2. Salat or obligatory prayer that is prescribed upon the believer. The Muslim must pray five daily prayers unless there are mitigating circumstances.
3. Sawm or fasting during the holy month of Ramadan. A Muslim must fast from sunrise to sunset for the duration of the holy month of Ramadan unless they are exempt. Fasting not only involves refraining from food and fluid, but it also involves being kind to others and refraining from saying or doing anything cruel that can cause harm to yourself and/or to others. We, as Muslims, are expected to behave in this exemplary manner 365 days a year, however, it is especially the case during the holy month of Ramadan. The importance of this cannot be overstated. Whilst it is true that what goes into your mouth can invalidate your fast, it is also true that what comes out of your mouth can also invalidate your fast.
4. Hajj or the pilgrimage to Mecca in Saudi Arabia (which draws an average of over 2 million people a year) during a defined period at least once in a lifetime for those who are able.
5. Zakat or almsgiving, which is donating a percentage of your income to charity.

Islam is, however, more than just a religion, it's a way of life that guides you to have harmonious relationships with God, yourself, others and the world about you. The two sources that Muslims draw their Islamic knowledge from are the Holy Quran (the sacred scripture that Muslims believe to be the infallible word of Allah) and the Hadith (the prophetic sayings and actions of the messenger Muhammad PBUH).

Muslims are not the only religious group who report that they find faith beneficial for their mental health. For me, my mental health deteriorated when I deviated from the path of Islam and it improved once I returned to it. For example, it is immensely comforting, even therapeutic, to know that Allah is the most merciful and that He will forgive us for all our sins (except for associating partners with Him, i.e., polytheism and idol worshipping) if we turn to Him in sincere repentance. As mortals we cannot impose limits on the mercy of Allah (this is considered a grave sin in Islam). Indeed, there is a famous Hadith that if you were to come to Allah with a mountain of sins, he will come to you with a mountain of forgiveness. All we need to do is turn to Allah and repent with sincerity.

When you are in the throes of a major depressive disorder and ruminating on all your sins, you can experience excessive guilt that can immobilise you. The knowledge that Allah is the most Merciful can short circuit that vicious rumination cycle that perpetuates the feeling of excessive guilt and help bring 'sakinah' tranquillity to your heart and mind. You subsequently stop punishing yourself. Many people who experience excessive guilt believe that they deserve to be punished for the sins they committed. This can include, but is not limited to, the refusal to receive treatment because they believe they don't deserve to get better; they deserve to continue suffering as a form of punishment for all their sinful deeds.

I find Islam beneficial for my mental health because it helps to bring structure, purpose and discipline into my life. Islam encourages me to be kind, grateful and compassionate towards my fellow human beings, Muslim and non-Muslim alike, and inspires me to serve society and help to protect the most vulnerable amongst us. I have never brought up my faith background in a clinical context in the United Kingdom. The NHS operates largely from a secular framework that tends to exclude spirituality and religiosity. That's not to say that there are no faith services available. The chaplaincy services in hospitals, for example, provide support to patients with health conditions, including mental health conditions. However, the content of psychotherapy for example, certainly in the NHS, is not faith-based or faith-informed. We must also be mindful, as mental healthcare professionals, that patients with mental health problems can often be vulnerable and suggestible. Topics like faith must be discussed carefully and cautiously and must NEVER be imposed on the patient, as perceived by them or otherwise. If ever I discuss the benefits of the Islamic faith for my mental health it is usually in a teaching or public speaking context and for the purposes of scholarship and research, as will be discussed later. The fields of Muslim mental health and Islamic psychology have emerged over the past two decades and the quantity of research being conducted in these areas is increasing. For example, the *Journal of Muslim Mental Health* is an interdisciplinary, peer-reviewed academic journal that publishes articles covering a wide range of topics that affect the mental health of Muslims worldwide including Muslim majority and Muslim minority countries. These topics include social sciences, culture, psychiatry, psychology, politics and theology.

It is deeply disturbing and distressing when the message of Islam is twisted and contorted by certain fanatics and zealots to support their deplorable and disgusting ideologies of violence and terrorism. Unfortunately, due to the rise of such terrorist organisations and the abhorrent acts that they have carried out in the name of Islam, Islamophobia has become a growing problem in the Global North.

According to the Center for American Progress, Islamophobia has been defined as, 'An exaggerated, irrational fear, hatred and hostility towards Islam and Muslims perpetuated by negative stereotypes resulting in bias, discrimination and marginalisation of Muslims from civic, social and political life'. Islamophobia has, however, become racialised; you do not have to be a Muslim to be a victim of Islamophobia, just having darker skin complexion can be enough. For example, many members of the Sikh community report they have been the victims of violent Islamophobic attacks. Perhaps this is one of the reasons that the British Government's All

Party Parliamentary Group on British Muslims convened and formulated the following working definition of Islamophobia, 'Islamophobia is rooted in racism and is a type of racism that targets expressions of Muslimness or **perceived** Muslimness'.

I have seen the devastating consequences of terrorist attacks perpetrated by the far right and by organisations who call themselves Muslims, outlined briefly later.

As I have mentioned, I used to live in Leeds in England. This is the place where the perpetrators of the heinous and horrific London 7/7 terror attacks were from. What drives individuals to commit such vulgar crimes against humanity? Many have pointed their accusing fingers towards religion and Islam. However, MI5 reports that

> *Far from being religious zealots, a large number of those involved in terrorism do not practise their faith regularly. Many lack religious literacy and could be regarded as religious novices. Few of them have been raised in strongly religious households, and there is a higher-than-average proportion of converts. Some are involved in drug-taking, drinking alcohol and visiting prostitutes [all haram (prohibited) in Islam]. There is evidence that a well-established religious identity actually protects against violent radicalisation . . . .*

The last sentence is definitely worth repeating; Islam is a factor that can protect against violent radicalisation.

In the case of the perpetrators of the abominable London bombings, terrorist organisations such as Daesh often prey on vulnerable disaffected Muslim youth who struggle with their identity. Not knowing how to integrate and/or not being accepted by society despite an individual's earnest efforts and a 'longing to belong' can increase an individual's vulnerability. What if you are raised in a society that makes you feel you are a nobody and that you will never amount to anything in life because of your race and the complexion of your skin? You turn to the online community for companionship and a recruiter from Daesh befriends you. Instead of rejecting you and putting you down, as has been the case for your entire youth, they not only accept you but they embrace you, elevate you and even glorify you. To be clear, there is *never, ever* any justification or excuse to carry out such barbaric acts of violence. But for us to know the solution to violent radicalisation, we must know what the factors are that contribute to this egregious problem. And the environment that a person is raised in is a factor that contributes to their behaviours.

I was fortunate to work as a junior psychiatrist (Psychiatry Registrar) in Hamilton, New Zealand from June 2016 to January 2017. Hamilton is a small city in North Island approximately 150 km away from Auckland. I loved living and working in New Zealand and I was particularly fond of the Māori people and culture. The Māori had spiritual relationships with nature – the land, rivers, and seas. Unfortunately, due to the legacy of colonialism they were and remain an oppressed people who are over-represented in the criminal justice system and acute mental healthcare services. The social determinants of health and criminal behaviours such as poverty and unemployment plague the Māori people and public health experts and criminologists will be amongst the first to tell you that there are policies that can help to reduce health inequalities and inequities and criminal behaviours, yet unfortunately the necessary political reform has not taken place.

In Māori culture, the elder plays a central role in the Whanau or family structure. It was touching to witness the Circle of Care meetings on the inpatient psychiatric wards that I used to work in at Waikato Hospital. The elder of the family was invited to offer a Karakia (Māori incantations and prayers) to invoke spiritual guidance and protection and to ward off malevolent spirits. Belief in Mākutu or witchcraft is not uncommon amongst the Māori people who would often attribute mental health disturbances to evil spirit possession. Such beliefs in supernatural causes were not considered delusional since they were consistent with religious or cultural norms.

Whilst working in New Zealand I was fortunate to deliver an oral presentation at the Royal Australian and New Zealand College of Psychiatrists Conference in Christchurch. My talk was about challenging mental-health-related stigma in healthcare professionals and students. Christchurch at the time was still healing and rebuilding from the devastating earthquakes that had occurred some years back. Nonetheless, the rebuilding didn't detract from the beauty of the place and I was captivated by the scenery whenever I would go for my morning runs before the conference.

One morning, before my run, I went to Al Noor Masjid, a mosque in Christchurch, and I offered my fajr or morning prayers there. There was nothing unusual about the mosque. It was like other mosques I have been blessed to pray in throughout the world. Although most of the mosques I've prayed in make you feel welcome, Al Noor Masjid was exceptional in this regard. It was the first and only time I prayed there but I instantly felt at ease and a valued member of the congregation and community. It's an ineffable feeling. Suffice to say though that praying in Al Noor Mosque was one of the highlights of my stay. As is custom in Islam, after offering your requisite prayers you greet the people you literally prayed side-by-side with and shake their hands. We smiled at each other, offered the greeting of salam or peace and exchanged pleasantries before going our own separate ways. This was back in October 2016 and everything in New Zealand was 'business as usual' or so it seemed to me. Nothing could have prepared me for the terrible event that would later occur in Al Noor Mosque on the 15 March 2019.

I had returned to the United Kingdom by then and I was giving a lecture about the treatment of Autism Spectrum Condition at a conference organised by the Royal College of Psychiatrists in York. I remember receiving a notification that a terrorist act had been perpetrated in New Zealand of all places – a nation that is regarded as one of the safest and most peaceful in the world. A white supremacist had stormed into Al Noor Mosque with military style semi-automatic weapons and had opened fire at Muslim worshippers who were offering their jummah or congregational Friday prayers at the mosque. A total of 51 of our fellow human beings – men, women, and children – were brutally murdered in this terrorist attack fuelled by hatred and Islamophobia. Even though I was in the United Kingdom, I could feel the reverberations of the attack. I remember after initially being in a state of shock and being unable to accept and believe what happened I passed out briefly. After regaining consciousness, I had to excuse myself from the conference and I went to the only place I thought I could go, the local mosque in York. The pain permeating throughout the masjid was palpable. We were all traumatised by the atrocity that was senselessly carried out against our Muslim brothers, sisters and children in Christchurch. I think many of us were anxious and afraid that there might be a copycat terrorist who would storm into the mosque and execute us in the same way as the Muslim worshippers in Al Noor Mosque were executed.

Suffice to say that I, like many others throughout the world who were not present and physically far removed from Al Noor Masjid, experienced psychological distress due to the attack. I cannot fathom the trauma, pain and suffering of those who were more intimately affected – who were at the masjid during the massacre and whose loved ones were brutally killed – must have gone through and indeed are still going through. When I teach medical students about how to develop empathy towards people living with mental health conditions I invite them to imagine what it must be like living with, for example, psychotic symptoms such as hearing voices and how people react towards you. I quote Atticus Finch from Harper Lee's timeless classic *To Kill a Mockingbird*, 'You never really understand a person until you consider things from his point of view – until you climb into his skin and walk around in it . . . .' But how do I climb into the skin of a person whose loved one was taken away from them so violently and so suddenly and in such a cruel manner? How do you imagine the unimaginable? Where do we even begin when attempting to heal the psychological wounds that the loved ones and survivors sustained from the atrocities? I'm not saying that those affected wouldn't benefit from receiving trauma-informed care or that they shouldn't seek it. But I don't think we can ever fully recover from such traumatic experiences; the wounds are just too deep.

What is an important contributor to convalescence is accountability. So long as the perpetrator of any type of trauma evades accountability that is bound to delay if not prevent the healing process. Forgiving the perpetrator is a different matter altogether. I don't think we should ever feel forced to forgive or that it makes us any less human if we choose not to. To forgive or not to forgive is a personal choice. Forgiveness can be restitutive for the victim and that, in my opinion at least, isn't selfish in the slightest. In other words, there is absolutely nothing wrong with choosing to forgive someone not for the sake of the perpetrator but entirely for your own sake and, sometimes, that can be for the sake of salvaging your own sanity.

The New Zealand Government later contacted me to review an application that they had received. The application was for funding to conduct research on the psychological consequences of the Christchurch mosque terror attacks. It was a robust proposal that included Patient and Public Involvement (PPI is an increasingly important metric in health research) at every level. The investigators also consulted Imams or Muslim leaders at the mosques in Christchurch to ensure the research would be sensitive and respectful towards the Islamic faith. I fully endorsed the proposal and the New Zealand Government authorised the allocation of funds for the research to be carried out.

I returned to the United Kingdom from New Zealand in January 2017. I had taken three years out of specialist training to deliver my anti-stigma talk, The Wounded Healer, to audiences throughout the world. I resumed my specialist training in psychiatry in February 2017 and after six-and-a-half long and difficult years (during which mental healthcare services and teaching and training had been rocked by a ruthless global pandemic) I finally obtained my Certificate of Completion of Training and entered the Specialist Register. I briefly worked as a Locum Consultant Psychiatrist in London (UK) before packing my bags and moving to London, Ontario in Canada.

I had visited London, Ontario, several times before migrating there. I was struck by how peaceful, inclusive, progressive and diverse the city was. I would frequent London Muslim Mosque (LMM) where I would pray the requisite prayers and participate in some of the mosque activities that included attending talks about youth empowerment and community engagement. LMM was everything that a mosque should be. It was a cultural hub where people in the local community met to socialise with one another and contribute to the betterment of society. The universal values of respect, kindness, trustworthiness and generosity were promoted by the mosque.

I would also have formal and informal meetings with the university and hospital staff who made me feel I was already a valued member of their teams. My positive experiences visiting London, Ontario, especially the mosque and the kind treatment I received from the hospital and university faculties influenced my decision to take the plunge and make the big move to Canada.

I remember that several years before I made the move to Canada, I had come across headlines on social media about the mass killing of a Muslim family residing in London, Ontario. I had a foreboding that the tragic incident was fuelled by Islamophobia, which reports would later confirm. On the 6 June 2021, in broad daylight in a peaceful residential neighbourhood, a far-right fanatic rammed his pick-up truck into a Canadian Muslim family of Pakistani descent, killing four and wounding a fifth. Just like that, three generations from the same family were murdered in cold blood. The sole survivor was rendered an orphan at the age of nine and must live with this unimaginable trauma for the rest of their life. I don't remember the global media taking that much of an interest in the story even though I would later learn that this monstrous Islamophobic attack was the deadliest mass killing in London's history. Would there be the same media reaction if the perpetrator was an 'Islamist' terrorist who had rammed his pick-up truck into a white Canadian family killing four and wounding a fifth?

There was, however, an outpouring of love, humanity and support from the people of London and Canada at large. A mass vigil was attended by thousands including the Prime Minister of Canada, Justin Trudeau. This was during the imposition of the Covid-19 restrictions of social distancing, however, these restrictions were temporarily lifted so that the vigil could proceed.

At a court appearance on the 10 June 2023, the perpetrator pleaded not guilty to charges, which included terrorism, and at the time of writing this book in October 2023, the trial is still ongoing. Many members of the local community have been re-traumatised by footage of the trial and the perpetrator's not guilty plea.

The Youth Coalition Combating Islamophobia (YCCI) was assembled in the wake of the terror attacks to challenge hatred in its many forms and to support a traumatised community. Having spoken with the parents of the younger people affected by the terror attack – including the lone survivor of the attack whose family members had been so brutally killed – they asked me to share my story about overcoming adversity at a forthcoming event as they felt it was important to convey messages of hope, recovery, healing and strength. The parents really emphasised the strength component of my story stating that many younger people feel like they have been weakened and immobilised by the atrocity. Unfortunately, the event has been delayed due to the atrocities occurring in Gaza.

My personal experiences of Islamophobia and my mental health being adversely affected by terrorism inspired me to pioneer a talk entitled, 'Canaries in a Coal Mine: Islamophobia and Muslim Mental Health'. In the talk I provide background information about the political landscapes in countries in the Global North (where anti-Muslim hatred is thriving), the rise of radicalisation and Islamophobia and how they have contributed to a toxic atmosphere in the Western world that is suffocating us all, Muslims and non-Muslims alike.

I describe how in the United Kingdom Islamophobia has stealthily infiltrated the provision of mental healthcare services under the guise of the British Government's controversial anti-radicalisation programme, Prevent. It is a statutory duty for healthcare workers to screen for signs of radicalisation in their patients and to report to the relevant authorities any patients they suspect may be vulnerable to violent extremism. The United Kingdom is the only country in the world where it is expected of a healthcare system to screen for radicalisation. Academics, human rights activists and reputable organisations such as the United Nations and politicians have expressed their collective outrage that Prevent has been made mandatory in healthcare systems. Prevent has been described by academics as an example of the securitisation of healthcare that operates under a surveillance framework, not a safeguarding framework, that, unsurprisingly, disproportionately affects Muslims. The People's Review of Prevent revealed that it was deeply Islamophobic and the authors of the report state, 'Prevent is discriminatory in its impact on Muslim communities. It is directed primarily at children and young people who make up around half of all referrals. This includes children at nursery and primary schools . . . Our report shows that Prevent involves serious potential breaches of Children's Rights and Human Rights . . . .'

Early in my training, I will never forget working one night shift as a doctor in Emergency Psychiatry. I had received an urgent call from colleagues in the Psychiatric Intensive Care Unit (PICU) where the most unwell mental health patients were being assessed and treated. Going to PICU is almost always a distressing experience not least because you witness first-hand how cruel, severe and devastating the symptoms of mental illness are, but you also see how it disproportionately affects communities of colour. On that particular shift, every single patient in PICU was a black man. For me, this illustrated the infiltration of racism in psychiatry. You are more likely to receive a psychiatric diagnosis of schizophrenia, for example, if you are black. You are four times more likely to be admitted into a psychiatric hospital involuntarily (i.e., detained under a Section of the Mental Health Act) if you are black. A factor that can contribute to the over-representation of black people – especially black men – in acute mental healthcare settings including PICU is that negative stereotypes are made about black men. For example, black men are often perceived as being violent. Violence is associated with schizophrenia. A black man may be passionate about vocalising his discontent. This could be the result of socioeconomic injustices that are rampant in his community because of certain policies. His discontent could also be about being the victim of police brutality and racism. Instead of being regarded as a social justice activist, he would be considered 'schizophrenic' and detained under the Mental Health Act. As absurd as that may sound, such stories are common.

The patient I was asked to review was 'behaving erratically' to the degree that the emergency response team had to physically restrain him, and they were drawing up powerful tranquilisers to chemically restrain him. I heard someone whisper behind me 'he's a terrorist' (the patient was holding a copy of the Holy Quran in his hand), however, I could not tell who it was who had said this. I immediately intervened and instructed my colleague to put the tranquilliser away and to allow me to speak with the patient. Noticing that he was holding a copy of the Holy Quran in his hand, I greeted him gently and respectfully with the greeting of salam, which is the Arabic word for peace. It was at that moment, I was later told, it was the first time the patient made eye contact with anyone. I asked him if he was a practising Muslim and he nodded his head. I then asked if reciting from the Quran was comforting for him and he again nodded his head. I suggested that he recite a passage of the Quran with me, surah Fatiha or the opening chapter, and he immediately nodded his head, opened the Quran to this page and together we recited this passage in unison. There was an instant transformation in his presentation with tears of joy streaming down his face. The situation de-escalated without the need for any chemical restraint and he soon went to sleep. This is one of many examples of how Islamophobia can infiltrate clinical practice and also how the Islamic faith can be beneficial for the mental health of Muslims.

In my anti-Islamophobia presentation, I make reference to the development and validation of the Perceived Islamophobia Scale by Professor Jonas Kunst and colleagues at the University of Oslo in Norway, which provides empirical evidence that Islamophobia is associated with psychological distress in Muslims and those perceived as Muslim. As mentioned before, Islamophobia has become racialised and as such you do not have to be a Muslim to be a victim of Islamophobia, just having darker skin colour is enough to be at the receiving end of anti-Muslim hatred.

To combat Islamophobia, there must be top-down and bottom-up approaches. An example of a bottom-up approach to combating Islamophobia is the 'Love a Muslim Day' that was organised by the non-governmental organisation Muslim Engagement and Development.

On 3 April 2018, anonymous letters were distributed to homes and businesses across the United Kingdom calling for people to participate in 'Punish a Muslim Day'. Muslim Members of Parliament were also sent the letter containing the violent threats. The letter depicted a points system whereby participants could win points for carrying out a range of hate crimes aimed at Muslims, the more violent the activity the more points the participant would score. For example, a participant would score 25 points for removing a headscarf from a Muslim woman and 1000 points for burning or bombing a mosque.

In a powerful example of how to combat hatred, the 'Love a Muslim Day' was launched that also followed a points system; however, participants would win points for carrying out acts of kindness towards Muslims, the kinder the gesture the more points the participants would score. For example, you would score 10 points for smiling at a Muslim and 1000 points for organising a fundraiser for the needy, especially those suffering in Muslim majority countries like Iraq, Libya and Kashmir. Of course, it will take more than such grassroots initiatives to defeat Islamophobia and 'Love a Muslim Day' did come under criticism by members of the Muslim community who would argue that it's another attempt to humanise Muslims and make us acceptable when really we should be asking and addressing why are we in this position in the first place. Such criticisms are not ill-founded or without any basis or validity. However, I and many other Muslims throughout the United Kingdom appreciated the display of love and solidarity shown towards us in response to the vitriolic attack fuelled by Islamophobia.

An example of how celebrities can combat Islamophobia is the 'Salah Effect'. Mohammed or 'Mo' Salah plays as a forward for Liverpool Football Club (LFC). Salah is regarded as one of the best footballers in the world.

Whenever Salah scored a goal for LFC he would celebrate by performing sujood, that is prostrating and placing his forehead on the ground. The sujood is a part of the Islamic prayer and by performing it on a world stage Salah was indicating that he is an adherent of the Islamic faith (i.e., he is a Muslim) and he is also expressing his gratitude to God for scoring the goal (the Moroccan National Football Team or the Atlas Lions would collectively perform the sujood in the 2022 FIFA World Cup in Qatar during their sensational campaign which saw them reach the semi-finals – the first African nation to have reached that knockout stage in a World Cup). So emblematic is Salah's sujood that the celebration is included in the video game FIFA 2019 played by millions throughout the world.

Football is the national sport in England and professional footballers have enormous influence and clout in British culture. Could Salah singlehandedly reduce Islamophobia and therefore racism in British society? A fascinating study conducted by the Immigration Policy Lab at Stanford University entitled, 'Can Exposure to Celebrities Reduce Prejudice? The Effect of Mohamed Salah on Islamophobic Behaviours and Attitudes.' In this study, a variant of the synthetic control method (a statistical method used to evaluate the effect of an intervention in comparative case studies) was employed to generate a counterfactual hate crime rate for the Merseyside Metropolitan County police force – which covers the city of Liverpool – after Salah signed for LFC in 2017. The authors revealed a causal effect of Salah joining LFC on Islamophobia through extracting and observing hate crime data from 25 police departments in England between 2015 and 2018. According to the authors, Merseyside Metropolitan County experienced a 16% lower hate crime rate after Salah was signed for LFC relative to the expected rate had he not been signed.

'The Salah effect' was also revealed through analysing over 15 million Tweets from UK football fans. The authors showed that LFC fans halved their rates of posting anti-Muslim Tweets (a drop from 7.3 to 3.8%) relative to fans of other top-flight English football clubs.

The authors of the report commented on this 'Salah Effect' and concluded that, 'The survey experiment suggests that these results may be driven by increased familiarity with Islam. . . These findings indicate that positive exposure to outgroup role models can reveal new information that **humanises** the outgroup at large . . . .' I also include the 'Salah Effect' in my anti-Islamophobia presentation, which is a highly effective way to engage students since many of them are fanatical about football.

It is heartening that my anti-Islamophobia talk has been integrated into the dental and medical school curricula of King's College London and Cambridge University. I have also delivered my anti-Islamophobia talk at events and conferences locally, regionally, nationally and internationally. For example, following the horrific attack at Pulse nightclub in Orlando, Florida on the 12 June 2016 by a terrorist who was identified as Muslim (but whose actions are antithetical to the teachings of Islam), there was unsurprisingly a spike in anti-Muslim hate crimes.

I was subsequently invited to deliver a Keynote lecture at a conference in Orlando to challenge Islamophobia. Other than the 'random' security check in Manchester Airport, it was an incredibly positive experience. It was the first time I had met 'Make America Great Again supporters'. Wearing their red caps, they would approach me one after the other thanking me for my talk.

Islamophobia, like other types of hatred such as anti-Semitism, is a scourge in our world that must be purged. It is a source of tremendous suffering and it can be deadly. Perpetrators of hate crimes such as terrorist acts ultimately aim to cause division. By standing in solidarity against hatred and promoting peaceful coexistence we can root out this evil from our world. Inter-group contact between a member of a group that is stigmatised and a member of a group that isn't stigmatised (i.e., between a Muslim and a non-Muslim in a country in the Global North) can help to reduce Islamophobia. After a terror attack Islamophobia can seemingly be ubiquitous, and studies have shown that such attacks adversely affect the mental health of Muslims.

It can be difficult to know where to start when challenging Islamophobia. My thought is that there is no better place to start than the human heart. You, as an individual, can make a difference. Are you going to perpetuate Islamophobia or are you going to be an agent of change and challenge it?

9

Dancing in the Dark

'You've been dancing in the dark.' That is what my best friend Wassim said to me before I created my Twitter (now X) account back in 2018. As I mentioned in a previous chapter, one of the main reasons I pioneered The Wounded Healer programme was to get the message of hope and recovery out there to as many people as possible. I had been travelling up and down the United Kingdom and indeed throughout the world and I was extremely fortunate to do so. This was hugely rewarding but it didn't come without its challenges. It was tiring and draining at times. And then came Tweeting.

I don't know why I waited for so long to join Twitter. Social media provided a platform to reach an even larger audience. I could connect with people all over the world without having to leave the house. Not that travelling isn't fun. On the contrary, one of the many benefits, privileges and joys of The Wounded Healer was that I got to travel nationally and internationally and nothing can ever replace face-to-face contact. But it was a lot easier to connect with people digitally, for me and for them, and that was especially advantageous for those who may not be able to leave their homes for health and/or other reasons.

It was great to be able to share my thoughts and feelings about all things mental health. I was able to share my story and learn about the stories of others who have also experienced mental health struggles. There was so much to share, learn and embrace. Twitter was also a space where the latest research articles on mental health would be posted, so this platform also helped increase my knowledge.

I remember starting off by posting content about a global mental health conference I attended. I took a picture of a slide from a PowerPoint presentation about the 'treatment gap' in low- and middle-income countries showing the number of psychiatrists there are per population. For example, in Zimbabwe there are 12 psychiatrists for a population of more than 16 million! These Tweets were getting some likes and so I continued posting mental health and psychiatry-related content.

I was slowly but surely building a following. However, the breakthrough moment occurred when I was working my first Emergency Psychiatry shift at St Thomas' Hospital in Westminster, Central London. The hospital is situated on the banks of the River Thames and you can see the Houses of Parliament and Big Ben. It was especially stunning at night when the lights are turned on and you can see their reflection and the reflection of the moon on the Thames. Just thinking about it now makes me nostalgic! The shifts in Emergency Psychiatry in St Thomas' Hospital were almost always difficult. The patients we would be asked to assess and treat were usually extremely unwell and they would attend with complex presentations. Because of the presence of multiple bridges in the area there were many patients we would see who attempted suicide by jumping from, for example, London Bridge into the River Thames and who would be hauled onto an Uber boat that would be patrolling the waters.

It was during a lunch break in the middle of my first shift there that I stumbled upon a Marks & Spencer Food Department in the hospital. I remember being immediately struck by what I saw and feeling overwhelmed by emotions as memories of when I first arrived in the United Kingdom at the age of 17 and working full time in M&S came flooding back. I remembered the 14-hour shifts I worked stacking shelves and filling fridges. I remember dreaming that one day I would become a doctor working in London saving lives and yet when I told colleagues at work about this dream, they made me feel like I was delusional and that it would never come true. And yet there I was, Dr Ahmed Hankir working a shift in Emergency Psychiatry providing care to suicidal patients at St Thomas' Hospital in Central London. My dream came true! I wanted to capture that moment and feeling and share it to let people from disadvantaged backgrounds know that they should never stop believing in themselves and that with hard work, forbearance and fortitude and God's grace upon us, we can realise our dreams.

I posted the Tweet with a selfie wearing an NHS lanyard standing in front of the M&S logo. The Tweet must have struck a chord because it went viral. I received over 100,000 likes from people all over the world. It was exhilarating. The Tweet caught the attention of some of the major media outlets including BBC World Services who later interviewed me about my journey. My following also increased considerably. I think I gained thousands of new followers. It was amazing! I got to connect with some incredible individuals who were so kind, positive and supportive. It's really very touching the comments they would make encouraging me and thanking me for my content and for my commitment to improving the lives of people living with mental health struggles.

I have since had a few posts go viral. I have noticed that the knowledge-based posts, as important as they are, don't really get many likes. It was the Tweets that revealed my journey, the obstacles that I had to overcome, the adversity, stigma, discrimination and racism that I faced, that really seemed to resonate. These were the Tweets that went viral.

I continue to post content about what I feel is beneficial for mental health like going for a walk in the woods or local lake or park or treating yourself to a cup of coffee (or cuppa to use the vernacular [for a cup of tea] in England!) in a quiet corner of your local cafe. I posted pictures of the beauty of nature and of the cafes in London that I frequented. I offered my personal thoughts, feelings and commentary about events on the news, especially stories related to mental health. I have even used Twitter/X to help raise funds for Palestinian children who were orphaned as a result of conflict, or the victims of the devastating floods in Pakistan or Libya. I post updates about my adventures (and misadventures!) travelling the world giving talks to the general public to reduce stigma and empower and dignify people living with mental health conditions and presenting the findings of my research at national and international conferences.

The responses and reactions have been overwhelmingly positive. I am now, at the point of writing this book, extremely blessed and fortunate to have a community of over 105,000 people on X. I have connected with like-minded and like-hearted people who feel just as passionately as I do about promoting mental health and preventing mental health problems.

I don't consider myself an influencer as such and I certainly don't identify as one. I have, however, been referred to as one. There will always be people who have a larger following and an even greater reach. I know of several doctors who have millions of subscribers on YouTube, TikTok, X, Instagram, for example. Most are based outside the United Kingdom. They have generated a large amount of revenue and have multiple streams of passive income as a result of their online activities. I think this does involve, to a degree, the monetisation of our attention and I can understand why some might feel uncomfortable with that. I personally have never monetised my content. That was never the reason for setting up an account. Not that I have anything against those who monetise their content. It's just not something I am interested in, certainly not at the moment. And to each their own.

There are many mental health advocates on social media who have been honest, open and transparent about their mental health experiences and I think that is fantastic. The more of us who share, the more we can reduce stigma. Of course, it's a personal choice and not everyone feels comfortable or ready to share. I think the most vocal community I have come across on X is the neuro-divergent one. I am immensely grateful to them for their insights and for raising awareness of the challenges they experience.

I think it is important to make a distinction between a mental health advocate and a mental healthcare professional. The former is usually a person living with a mental health condition or someone who is interested in mental health. The latter is a trained professional who has obtained qualifications and credentials after years (and years!) of specialist training and passing rigorous exams. To emphasise, it is important and necessary to amplify the voices of people living with mental health conditions. However, it is also important and necessary not to conflate a mental health advocate with a mental healthcare professional; the latter has acquired expertise through erudition and scholarship and the acquisition of knowledge and often from research they have conducted. It is true that mental health advocates are often 'experts by experience', that is, persons living with a mental health condition and the wisdom, insights and experiences they have gained from living with their condition is precious. That's why it is critical to involve people living with mental health conditions in the design, development and delivery of mental healthcare services and in mental healthcare policy. 'Experts by experience' must also play a leading role in stigma reduction initiatives. However, mental health advocates do not have specialist knowledge as a result of specialist training and qualifications. I think it is important to be clear about this as I have seen major media outlets invite mental health advocates to their studios and ask them questions that they would not know the answers to unless they have specialist knowledge. I do think it's important that mental health advocates living with a mental health condition have a platform to share their stories and insights about services, examples of good practice, and how services can improve. However, it is important that the audience becomes more educated about the difference between deferring to an advocate over a professional.

There are many psychiatrists on X including professors and presidents of the RCPsych, the American Psychiatric Association and the Royal Australian and New Zealand of Psychiatrists who are better placed to answer questions that require specialist knowledge. However, I do not think that we as a profession are showing leadership in the social media spaces and therefore these places are being occupied by those who are less qualified and less knowledgeable who, although they mean well, can potentially misinform, mislead and disinform the public – the consequences of which can be serious at best and harmful at worst.

I think sharing your mental health struggles on social media can be helpful. For example, I noticed a student on X who is honest, open and transparent about living with a severe mental illness. They were posting content whilst experiencing psychotic symptoms including paranoid and persecutory beliefs and auditory hallucinations. They were so unwell that they were admitted into hospital involuntarily and detained under a Section of the Mental Health Act. They subsequently received an outpouring of love, kindness, support and gifts sent to them from their X community. And rightfully so; people living with severe mental illness are no less deserving than those living with a severe physical illness of empathy and compassion. However, if you visit the psychiatric wards, you will see they are bereft of cards and gifts (whereas physical health wards are full of them). I am in full support of people sharing but I think we must be careful and cautious, especially when acutely unwell. We might post content that we will later regret that we cannot erase because it isn't a true reflection of who we are.

When I was forced to interrupt medical school due to the severity of the symptoms of my mental health condition, I didn't have any online presence. I didn't receive an outpouring of love, kindness and support. I certainly didn't receive any gifts. I think if I had, that would definitely have contributed to my recovery and would have had positive effects on my mental health. Instead, I was isolated, lonely, stigmatised and dehumanised. These things only made matters worse for me, prolonging my illness and hampering my recovery.

I think about the countless people living with mental health conditions – the symptoms of which are so severe that their minds are unable to receive or conceive ideas. Their thoughts might be so accelerated they are simply unable to keep up with them let alone vocalise them. Or there might be an absence or poverty of thought manifesting as 'alogia', the inability to speak. We never know about them, their suffering and struggling, their trials and tribulations, because we never hear from them because they are unable to talk – through no fault of their own – due to the severity of their symptoms. Often, they are unable to eat or drink and they become malnourished and emaciated. We don't notice them on our feeds on social media; it might be that they are too unwell to have a digital presence. They might be admitted into a psychiatric ward involuntarily or they could be suffering in silence in the community. They remain obscure to us and we will never know about them. But that doesn't mean they are any less deserving of our attention, kindness and compassion and certainly no less deserving of our gifts. Our hearts and prayers go out to them. It is scandalous to say the least that the government has failed people living with severe mental illness so spectacularly. They don't deserve this.

I didn't really think about the downside of social media. I was fully aware about online bullying and harassment, especially amongst younger people and how that contributed to suicidal behaviours. I saw it firsthand in my day-to-day practice, especially in emergency psychiatry settings. But prior to joining Twitter in 2018, I hadn't experienced any online abuse because up until then I didn't really have an online presence. For some reason it didn't cross my mind and I didn't think I would be affected or targeted. How wrong I was!

No matter how hard you try not to offend or upset anyone or how careful you are, it seems like online abuse is inevitable, especially if you 'put yourself out there'. There have been multiple times when people have posted negative content aimed at me. At the early stages of my development, I would just block them. I soon learned there were better ways to manage the negativity. Also, with blocking, which was a reaction to the negativity I received, the perpetrators of that negativity would take a screenshot and concoct a narrative that would frame themselves as the victim and me as the aggressor for blocking them without providing any contextual information. That said, I was still learning and with the benefit of hindsight and experience I realised there were better ways to deal with negativity. That's not to say that you shouldn't consider blocking others – it's a personal choice – especially when it comes to protecting your energy and your mental health. Normalise doing whatever it takes to protect your energy and your mental health. Just be prepared for the person you blocked to frame themselves as the innocent victim and you as the aggressive villain. I'm reminded of this Tweet I came across but I can't remember the name of the person who posted it, 'Funny how you become the villain when you become more assertive.'

You will soon begin to recognise patterns. In other words, you will identify the people who either say negative and horrible things about you or who 'like' negative and horrible things about you. For example, I often don't even have to read a Tweet to know if it's negative or not; I can tell by who has liked that Tweet. If that person has an obsession with posting or liking negative Tweets about me, I can predict, with reasonably high accuracy, that the Tweet they liked was negative. I personally think that's a shame and that there are far better things to do with your time than post or like negative Tweets. There are also the people on Twitter who NEVER engage with your positive content but the moment they see a crack or an opportunity to bring you down they will pounce upon you without any hesitation, restraint or remorse. Normalise distancing yourself from those who devote their time searching for faults in others. I also find that these people are quick to criticise others but are not receptive to criticism themselves. Also be wary of those who criticise you and frame it as 'constructive' when everything they said was utterly destructive.

I think the most toxic people are the ones who attack you and then frame it as if the fault is with you and how you reacted. There is a term for that; it's called gaslighting. You don't need that toxicity in your life, so normalise distancing yourself from perpetrators of that toxicity. I don't think it's healthy and helpful to be defensive all the time. I think we should be receptive to criticism. But we should also be respectful to one another. The 'keyboard warriors' seem to struggle with this. I remember one particular keyboard warrior. He happened to be a colleague, a fellow psychiatrist I worked side-by-side with. I was never negative towards him in person or online. For some reason he decided to attack me on social media. I saw him in person for the first time at the workplace after the online attacks. There was nothing warrior-like about him, certainly when he wasn't behind his screen. Instead, he was very awkward. He didn't say anything. He managed to avoid me. I think he was ashamed; so he should have been.

Unfortunately, the worst attacks have come from fellow psychiatrists. There were two attacks on Twitter in particular that were so harmful and vitriolic that if I was not so resilient, the online abuse would have been enough to make me suicidal. These direct attacks on me were from members of a profession that has been charged with protecting my mental health and preventing suicide. That is why to this day such behaviour online from mental healthcare professionals shocks and astonishes me. It is inconceivable in my mind that any person who conducts themselves in this manner online, in person or in any other context, can be a mental healthcare professional. There is absolutely nothing professional or caring about attacking people online. Mental healthcare professionals, of all people, should know better. They should know that such attacks are harmful for mental health and can contribute to suicidal behaviours. There is an oath that all doctors have taken to do no harm and a code of conduct that we should all follow. A reason why online abuse persists and appears to be worsening is because there is no accountability. Perpetrators instead are not only 'rewarded' with likes but are also seemingly rewarded by their profession. The current measures in place are not good enough. More must be done to hold perpetrators of online abuse to account, especially mental healthcare professionals, and more specialist support must be made available to victims. Tech companies must play a role in this but regulatory bodies and employers must also play a role. Otherwise, such perpetrators of online abuse will continue to post content that is harmful to mental health, the consequences of which can be fatal.

I don't want to end this chapter on a negative note. That would not do justice to all the incredible people I have connected with on social media and the outpouring of love, kindness and support I have received from them that far outweighs the negativity. I can't thank these people enough for their positivity and for all the encouragement they have given me. Social media can be an unforgiving place but it is ultimately a force for good. Social media provides a platform to people living with mental health conditions to amplify their voices who otherwise would have been silenced. It is the modern-day equivalent of the town hall where we can vocalise our views and challenge social injustices and raise awareness about health inequalities and inequities and inspire action to resolve these issues through advocacy and campaigning. It is a place where kindness can flourish, where you can connect with like-minded and like-hearted individuals. That social connectedness can literally be lifesaving. I have received messages from people telling me that although I don't know them and have never met them, my content is helping them and even saving lives. So don't be deterred or intimidated. Share your story of survival, spread your message of hope and recovery. And always remember, in a world where we can be anything, be kind.

10
Reframing

Specialist training in psychiatry in the United Kingdom usually involves two stages. The first stage is called 'Core Training' and, if working full-time, this usually takes three years to complete. Core Training comprises six placements in the different subspecialities of psychiatry with each placement lasting 6 months in duration. So, for example, the subspecialities in psychiatry that I worked in during my core training upon my return from New Zealand were Intensive Community Services (ICS) for Older People, Acute Male Adult Inpatient Ward, Assertive Outreach Team, Intellectual Disability Inpatient Ward, Liaison Psychiatry, Community Drug and Alcohol Addiction Services, and Acute Female Adult Inpatient Ward. The first two-and-a-half years of my Core Training were in Leeds (from February 2017 to August 2019), before I transferred to London.

My first placement in Intensive Community Services included working in the Memory Treatment Clinic assessing and providing care to older people with memory problems. It was and remains one of the most enjoyable placements I've ever worked in. I met older patients in the clinic, and they would share their fascinating life stories, their tales of adventure and misadventure, with me. There really is no greater privilege than that granted when a patient trusts and confides in you.

The patients open to the Memory Treatment Clinic were of a certain generation. This was way, way before the digital age and social media. Patients came with their partners, and we would talk about how and when they first met. 'I met her on the dance floor, and it was love at first sight!' It was touching. Often, couples had been married for decades and the romantic love they had for each other did not diminish. On the contrary, it was visible and palpable.

When a man, for example, revealed that he was born and raised in the region I would ask, 'So you are a Yorkshire man?' They would always emphatically and proudly reply, 'I most certainly am!' And rightfully so. You should be proud of your identity.

The generation that most of the patients at the Memory Treatment Clinic belonged to was affected by World War II one way or another and it was genuinely captivating to listen to how their lives were touched. A father of a patient, for example, may have tragically died in the trenches of Normandy. Or, depending how old they were, they may have served in World War II themselves. I remember meeting an older patient in a residential home who was a centenarian. Like other centenarians, she received a letter from the monarch, who at the time was Queen Elizabeth II, on her one- hundredth birthday. Also, next to the letter was a black and white picture in a frame of a young and rather dashing man in uniform. I looked at the lady whilst she was laying in her bed, who had a diagnosis of severe dementia, and politely asked if the handsome man in the picture was her husband and she wouldn't stop giggling! The support staff said that the man in the picture was indeed her husband and that despite having passed away many years ago, she was still very much in love with him. Such were the privileges and pleasures of working in later-life psychiatry.

Patients referred to our service usually had memory problems and they would receive a full psychiatric assessment and have the relevant tests and investigations before we would arrive at a diagnosis. Patients and their loved ones almost always wanted to know if the cause behind their problems was dementia. One of the neuropsychological tests we used to identify cognitive impairment in conditions such as dementia was the Addenbrooke's Cognitive Examination or ACE. Administering ACE involved asking the patient a series of questions and inviting them to complete activities to assess different cognitive domains such as attention, memory, language and visuo-spatial processing.

The results of each activity in each domain are scored to give a total score out of 100. The score must be interpreted with caution and in the context of the patient's overall history and examination, but a score of 88 and above is considered normal; below 83 is abnormal; and between 83 and 87 is inconclusive. The more severe the symptoms that the patient suffers from, the lower the score they receive. Dementia is a cruel condition that can wreak havoc in the lives of those suffering from it and their loved ones. It is a disease that usually gets progressively worse and the more advanced it is, the more severe the symptoms tend to be. There is no 'cure' for dementia; however, medications have been developed to help 'slow down' disease progression.

However, just because a patient received a low total score on the ACE tool, it doesn't necessarily mean that the quality of their life will also be low. I remember assessing a patient who attended the Memory Treatment Clinic with his wife. He had been referred to the service by his GP who, in the referral letter, suspected the patient may be developing dementia and hence they requested a specialist assessment. They were the loveliest couple, and the patient was just bursting with life! He was so upbeat and positive. It reminds me of this quote from the film *The Shawshank Redemption*, 'I guess it comes down to a simple choice, really. Get busy living, or get busy dying.' I was, therefore, quite surprised, when after administering the ACE tool on him he had a very low total score. I shared the result with the patient and his wife, and I will never forget his reaction. He didn't want to have regular follow-ups and multiple tests and investigations and to be started on any medications. Both he and his wife were 'perfectly happy'. I was not able to detect a trace of distress, dysfunction or 'danger' (patients with dementia can be a danger to themselves and/or others when, for example, they forget to take a pan off the cooker which can pose a fire hazard, or if they wander the streets at night). We therefore co-created a care plan whereby the service would have a follow-up appointment with the patient in six months. In the interim if there were any concerns or worsening in his condition then he and his wife could contact us and we could arrange a review appointment sooner. This is what the patient and his wife wished for and preferred and his satisfaction with the plan was such that he had a big smile on his face, and he shook my hand warmly before bidding me farewell.

There is another patient I'll never forget who was referred to the Memory Treatment Clinic. He was a man in his early 60s who was really struggling at work and at home with his family and this was causing him and his loved ones a great deal of distress. When I took a detailed psychiatric history from him, it became apparent just how much he was struggling. However, I was surprised when, after administering the ACE tool on him, he received a 'normal' score. This emphasises the point that the ACE score must be interpreted in the context of the patient's overall history and examination. These two examples illustrate there are many factors that can contribute to a person's quality of life. Of course, memory problems can be devastating, and we must be caring, empathetic and kind to all those who suffer from these symptoms. Distress, after all, is deeply subjective. But we shouldn't come to any conclusions about a person's quality of life and how they are coping based on the scores of neuropsychological tests in isolation, or if they are experiencing symptoms, or if they have been labelled or diagnosed with a health condition. Giving them a chance, hearing them out, respecting their preferences, wishes and autonomy are some of the most important lessons I learned whilst working in the Memory Treatment Clinic.

Still Alice is a 2014 US drama that powerfully portrays the devastating fragmentation of memory caused by Alzheimer's dementia and how this can destroy the lives of those suffering from this neurodegenerative disorder and the lives of the loved ones. The film stars Julianne Moore who plays the protagonist, a university professor who develops dementia. Moore garnered an Academy Award for Best Actress in a Leading Role for her sensational performance that faithfully captured how the debilitating symptoms of dementia can ruin lives but also the tremendous strength, dignity, courage and resolve that people living with the condition have.

Moore intensively and painstakingly researched Alzheimer's disease for months and she even had multiple meetings and discussions with people suffering from this condition to ensure that the depiction of the symptoms – and the impact they had on the lives of those affected – was accurate. There was one scene in the film that was particularly poignant. An academic conference was taking place in New York City where Moore's character and her family lived. The conference was attended by psychiatrists from the United States and beyond, including the psychiatrist that was providing care to Moore's character. The talks were almost entirely about the latest developments and research findings in dementia. Moore's character, however, was invited to give a talk about her experiences living with Alzheimer's disease. It is no exaggeration to state that it is one of the most moving scenes in cinematic history, certainly in my opinion. Moore's character evocatively and eloquently describes the debilitating effects that the symptoms of Alzheimer's disease have on her life and the lives of her family. She had to use notes and a felt tip pen to highlight the lines she read because of the memory problems she developed as a result of her condition. There was a moment when her notes fell to the floor and created a scene when she tried to collect and organise them. The audience, wanting to help but not knowing how and what to say or do, were stunned into silence and there was a palpable tension in the air. Moore's character, however, was able to masterfully dissolve it by employing humour, grace and dignity when she quipped with a sweet smile on her face, 'We will forget that happened!' and everyone burst into laughter. *Still Alice* and other similar films help to reduce stigma and humanise people living with, for example, Alzheimer's disease.

On the other end of the life continuum, I once provided care to a younger patient in a mental health crisis, whilst I was working in Emergency Psychiatry in Yorkshire, that I will never forget. The younger person had presented to emergency services after taking a mixed overdose of paracetamol and ibuprofen. They had been stockpiling and had taken enough medications to warrant infusion of an antidote.

A psychiatric history revealed the patient had been abandoned by their biological parents when they were a child and had been adopted by another family member at the age of seven. Since being adopted, the patient was repeatedly raped by that family member. Finally, they had the courage to report the perpetrator to the school who then reported this to the Police. The perpetrator was convicted and imprisoned for the crimes they committed. However, the family, instead of supporting the patient, blamed them for what had happened. The patient internalised this blame and was consumed by guilt.

I read in a book many years ago (which unfortunately I can't remember the title of) that there is a difference between knowing something and feeling something and it resonated deeply with me on personal and professional levels. In psychiatry, another way of articulating this would be there is a difference between internalising a message (in therapy for example) cognitively and emotionally. For example, people can repeatedly say to you that, 'It's not your fault' and you can believe them. You know in your mind that it is not your fault, but it still feels in your heart that it is your fault, and you continue to punish yourself.

Health and social care professionals continued to tell the patient that it was not their fault but the words, no matter how sincere they were and how frequently they were uttered, had no effect on this patient. The patient may have known what happened was not their fault but nonetheless felt that it was. This discrepancy between knowing something and feeling something can render a person vulnerable to suicidal behaviours. The aim of therapy, one could argue, is to align and harmonise your thoughts and feelings, so that, for example, you can both know and feel that it is not your fault.

I remember being a 'man on a mission' upon returning to the United Kingdom and resuming my specialist training in psychiatry. I didn't forget the humiliation I endured and the mistreatment, to use a euphemism, I received. I was energised and inspired. I set a goal: I would do whatever it took to win the RCPsych Core Trainee of the Year Award'. As I mentioned previously, the RCPsych Awards mark the highest level of achievement in psychiatry in the United Kingdom. I had previously won the RCPsych Foundation Doctor of the Year Award, however, I was even more driven to win the RCPsych Core Trainee of the year Award. It was a relentless year during which I published 13 research papers in peer-reviewed journals, and I presented at conferences and events nationally and internationally including Orlando, Berlin, Dublin and Sydney. My hard work paid off and sure enough by the grace of God I won the RCPsych Core Trainee of the Year award! To be honest, I was confident that I would, but I don't think my confidence was unfounded. I had worked tirelessly and relentlessly throughout the year going above and beyond the call of duty and I had made many sacrifices. It was an unforgettable experience to receive the award at a ceremony at the College Headquarters in London. I arrived late through no fault of my own (or was it Divine Intervention?). I had notified the College and they were very understanding. The Master of Ceremony was a BBC presenter and she decided to go 'off the script' when announcing that I was the winner in my category.

The RCPsych awards had different categories for teams and individuals. For example, there was Core Trainee of the Year, Higher Trainee of the Year, Psychiatrist of the Year, Community Mental Health Team of the Year, Inpatient Mental Health Team of the Year. For each winner, the MC would only read a summary of their achievements and why the judging panel selected them. However, as the MC later said to me, I was the exception. Whilst waiting for me to arrive, she read my entire list of achievements and successes. Not only that, she asked the audience to give me a standing ovation and to create a raucous reception for me! And that's exactly what happened! I remember being so delighted and jubilant that I skipped to the stage where the awards were being presented! It was a deeply dignifying and empowering experience, not least because I am certain that the minority of psychiatrists who are not supportive towards me (like the ones who humiliated and wounded me when I was interviewed for an academic post in the 'prestigious' institutions all those years ago) were there. I was defiant in the face of such prejudice and discrimination. It was my way of saying to them. 'You are wrong! I know my value and worth. You can't stop me from achieving my goals, establishing and making a name for myself, realising my dreams, and encouraging others, if they choose to embrace their vulnerability and be honest and open about their mental health struggles.' Work hard and with integrity, be kind and caring and giving and humble, and, most importantly, never stop believing in yourself.

I was and remain immensely grateful for the support I received and the positive reaction from many of my colleagues. However, there were people who weren't happy for me and who refused to recognise my achievement – receiving a national award which I thought would reflect positively for the region – let alone celebrate it. The following day there was an event taking place where psychiatrists across all grades and stages in the region were invited to attend. A senior figure kicked off proceedings by paying tribute to the doctors who received regional and national awards. The doctors who received the Core Trainee of the Year and Higher Trainee of the Year awards for the region were announced and invited to the stage to receive their certificates. There was a huge round of applause for both and rightfully so. Such recognition is important I feel because it helps to make you feel included and valued. It just so happened that the RCPsych Higher Trainee of the Year Award winner was also from the region (although for reasons that escape me, they didn't receive the regional award in this category). The senior figure paid tribute to her, 'One of our very own receiving a prestigious national award!' and the entire room gave her a standing ovation. And that was it. There was no mention whatsoever of my name and that I, too, had received a 'prestigious national award'. It was impossible that the senior figure wasn't aware that I had won this award. I was deliberately not included, recognised, and celebrated. Was I not, 'One of our own' like the other doctor who won the prestigious national award? If so, why not? I, too, was a doctor training in psychiatry in the region, like the other doctors who received a national award and who was recognised and celebrated in the regional event. It was from that moment that I sensed something wasn't right. It was as if people were suspicious of my success. Reaching the heights of mediocrity was as far as I could go as far as they were concerned; anything above and beyond that must be the result of foul play or an unfair advantage.

I remember coming under the cosh once when I posted a Tweet that I once suffered from severe symptoms of a mental health condition that reduced my life expectancy, then I transformed my lifestyle, and I am now able to run 15 km per day. I could have worded it better, but I certainly didn't intend to upset anyone by it. The relentless attacks that ensued were ruthless. Psychiatrists who I never met before started accusing me of fabricating that I ever experienced a severe mental health condition. They spoke with so much conviction even though they knew nothing about me. It was astonishing. One psychiatrist even stooped to say that my post was dangerous without even substantiating such a serious claim. It's as if he was saying, 'You can't succeed if the symptoms of your mental health condition are severe. You should aim and settle for surviving.' My response to that would be what type of message are you trying to get across? That people with a severe mental illness can't recover, thrive and achieve excellence? If that is the message you are trying to get across, you are the one being dangerous, not me!

Following the regional event I felt like I was under surveillance and that my movements were being monitored. It was the most horrible feeling. Although I delivered talks nationally and internationally and I was conducting research, teaching and publishing articles in academic journals, all this occurred in my own time either whilst on leave, during the weekends or before and after work. My commitment to patient care never faltered, as evidenced in all my clinical and educational supervisor reports. On the contrary, there was abundant evidence in my professional development portfolio to prove that I was consistently exceeding expectations when it came to my clinical performance.

There are two examples of many that stood out the most to me that were evidence to prove that I was being scrutinised unfairly. One weekday, I attended a weekly teaching session at the university as part of the training scheme. During this teaching session, I received a phone call informing me that a relative was admitted into hospital. So, I excused myself after lunch and went to visit them in the afternoon to make sure it wasn't anything serious (thank God it wasn't). I didn't think about it anymore. A few weeks later, I received an email from someone higher up the chain of command saying that they didn't see my signature on the signing-in sheet for the afternoon teaching session at the university. I replied immediately and gave them my reason and again I thought that would be the end of that. However, to my surprise they asked me to meet with a senior figure to discuss my absence further, which I thought wasn't necessary, but I attended the meeting anyway. During the meeting I just repeated what I said in my email and the senior figure didn't seem satisfied with my response and kept on probing and prying. I sensed something was untoward, but my 'statement' remained the same because it was the truth. He was eventually satisfied with my reason, ostensibly at least, and I said goodbye and left his office.

On my way home on the bus I received a call from a withheld number, and it was the senior figure with whom I had only just met. He sounded disturbed as if some calamity had happened. Apparently, there was an article that was obscurely concealed in the depths of the internet that they somehow managed to dig out after searching for God knows how long. It was about a talk that I had given on the day that there was the weekly teaching session that I partially missed because I went to the hospital to visit my relative. The accusation was that I skipped mandatory teaching to give this talk, thus confirming their suspicions that I had received the national award through some type of foul play or unfair advantage.

I was stunned by the perceived allegation, and I experienced an episode of amnesia partly because I felt that I had been set up and that the entire scenario had been contrived. Also, I had given countless talks and I genuinely couldn't remember the specific talk they were referring to. A few weeks had elapsed since then during which I had given several other talks. He asked me to return to his office immediately and so I did. On the way back to the office I remembered what had happened. I did indeed give a talk at that event on the day of the teaching session at the university which started at 8.00 pm. Before accepting the invitation, I made sure there were seats available on the 5.15 pm train service from Leeds to London where the event was taking place (it was only a 2-hour train journey to the capital). Teaching at the university finished at 5.00 pm so I went ahead and booked the ticket and informed the organisers I could accept their invitation. However, I had to excuse myself after lunch because my relative was admitted into hospital. After checking upon my relative and making sure she was safe, stable and comfortable I managed to leave the hospital just in time to catch the train. I explained all of this to the senior figure to which he replied, 'Did you keep the tickets of the train journey and if so, can you show them to me?' To which I responded no I didn't. At this point I thought this is getting ridiculous now and I am feeling violated. It became clear that this wasn't me being paranoid – they were clearly out to get me.

Another regional conference was organised; however, in this event, a senior figure contacted me and asked if I could give a talk. To be honest, I was taken aback. I was made to feel like I shouldn't be giving these talks, even though the feedback I was receiving from people who attended them was exceptionally positive with many stating that my talks were beneficial for their mental health – even lifesaving. I accepted the request and went to the event. Whilst there, I bumped into another senior figure who I knew had something against me. They refused to look at me, no words were exchanged between us, and we went our separate ways. I later gave the talk, and it went well with those who attended. That very night I received an email from the senior figure who, I saw at the event, and they said to me they didn't receive a 'study leave form' to attend the conference. I was shocked to receive this email both because of the timing (it was a Friday night) and because of the content. I actually felt really guilty, as if I had committed some unforgivable crime.

The following week I bumped into a colleague with whom I was on friendly terms and whom had also attended the event. He asked me how I was doing, and I told him I wasn't so great. I explained what had happened. I'll never, ever forget his reaction. He stared at me and said, 'What do you mean? I attended the event and I didn't fill out the form. Nobody who attended the event filled out a form.' I just looked at him in disbelief. Unlike me, he didn't even give a talk at the event, however, he didn't need to fill out a form so what about me, why should I fill the form out as an invited speaker? I was clearly being bullied.

It is perhaps unsurprising then that when I saw a post for an academic psychiatry position being advertised in London, I jumped at the chance. To cut a long story short, I submitted the application, was invited for an interview and received a job offer. It is superfluous to add that I accepted the offer immediately. At the exit meeting I had with my employer before moving to London, they were desperate to pin something against me to support their narrative that I was the problem and that they were not being prejudicial against me. However, as I mentioned before, my clinical and educational supervisor reports were flawless. They therefore had to resort to fabrication in their last-ditch efforts to discredit me. I couldn't have survived another moment in that toxic environment. It had become too damaging, and it was compromising my wellbeing. To my immense relief, I left the following day for London to start my new post and a new beginning. It wasn't a moment too soon. I had been treated like an animal in a cage. The moment I saw an opening, I escaped. I felt like a human again.

II

Firefighting

Upon relocating to London there wasn't any time to waste, and I got straight to work the following day. You could immediately notice and feel the huge change in the environment. The capital was bigger, faster and more diverse. In short, it was better and I felt that it was definitely an upgrade to the city I had been living in before. I can't deny it, I was excited!

During the induction period we received lectures from world leaders in the fields of psychiatry, psychology and neuroscience. The hospitals and the university I was working in were steeped in history and tradition and I felt privileged and honoured to be a part of them. I remember after a lecture had been given, the cohort of August 2019 – the group of doctors specialising in psychiatry in southeast London I had joined – gathered to take a picture. There must have been 50 of us at least. I recognised a few of the doctors. One of the 'core trainees' (as we were called) had attended my The Wounded Healer talk in Manchester way back in 2014 when she was a medical student and she remembered me from all those years ago. It was always a lovely feeling when someone approached me saying that they had attended one of my talks and benefited from it. I like to think that by sharing my recovery journey with them in a teaching and training context, I had positively influenced their personal and professional lives and that their views and attitudes towards people living with mental health conditions improved as a result. Would they be that bit kinder, that bit more empathetic, that bit more thoughtful and that bit gentler towards their patients with mental health problems? I certainly hope so.

I remember standing in the periphery in one of the back rows when the picture was taken. You wouldn't have even noticed me unless I was pointed out. There I am, hiding behind my colleagues leaning slightly to one side so that I am not entirely obscured. I think this was deliberate to a degree; a part of me wanted to be in the background. But a part of me also wanted to be seen, felt and heard, and to leave my mark.

The clinical placement I was working in was the Community Drug and Alcohol Addiction service in Brixton, which was situated in the London borough of Lambeth. Brixton was a cultural melting pot with a substantial proportion of people from Afro-Caribbean backgrounds. The diversity of the communities in Brixton was reflected in the fusion of the aromas emanating from the local restaurants. It was a foodie's paradise. You name it, there was a restaurant in Brixton that served it: jerk chicken, tikka masala, lamb shawarma. The mixture of the scents was tantalising, especially during lunch breaks. Instead of going for a 'meal deal' in the local supermarket we'd often head to one of the restaurants instead!

Unfortunately, the stench of cannabis also permeated and the sight of the people who smoked this drug and took other illicit substances, the pipes, syringes and paraphernalia they carried around with them, was heartbreaking and betrayed the pernicious problems in these areas. Social and societal ails such as domestic abuse, racism, poverty and unemployment can render a population vulnerable to homelessness and civil unrest. The reality can be so unbearable that many unsurprisingly resort to taking street drugs as a maladaptive means of escapism. These ails and the police brutality that communities of colour experience are perhaps some of the factors that contributed to the Brixton riots in the early 1980s. These issues to a large degree continue to plague the local communities in Lambeth. Unfortunately (or fortunately depending on how you look at it i.e., from a job security perspective), I wasn't going to be out of work anytime soon.

Although work was extremely busy, I was immensely happy as I couldn't have joined a better team. I felt included, valued and supported. I think this reflected the outstanding leadership from the consultant psychiatrist I was working for at the time. He was a worldly person who was flowing with knowledge about his subspecialty of addiction psychiatry but also more broadly about sociopolitical issues and current affairs. He knew more about the Middle East and Lebanon than I did, and he was Irish! I didn't feel bullied and harassed by him or any other member of the team and I didn't feel like I was under surveillance like I did in my previous post. This was London; there were so many high achievers I didn't stick out from the crowd. I think, more importantly however, that my line manager (i.e., my consultant) was very secure in himself and was not threatened by my successes, and he certainly didn't view it with any suspicion. The importance of this for my mental health, wellbeing and career progression cannot be overstated. It was a living hell in my previous post, always having this sense that I was being monitored and I would be pounced upon if I made the slightest 'mistake'. No, in London and in this placement I was emancipated from the shackles of unfounded suspicion, and I was in an environment where I could thrive clinically and academically.

I am reminded of another placement I worked in that had a culture of promoting microaggressions instead of microaffirmations. I had experienced a traumatic incident in my personal life, and it was no exaggeration to say that I was a 'doctor in distress'. A senior figure who, according to his profile, had a special interest in 'doctors in distress' bullied me. As a result, I really suffered and struggled. However, the moment I rotated to a different placement where, instead of being harassed, I felt supported and valued, my performance improved considerably, and I flourished. 'Make no mistake', I once Tweeted, 'the culture and environment we work in can profoundly affect our wellbeing and occupational functioning.' This, unfortunately, must have resonated with many users since the Tweet garnered over 5000 likes.

It was during my placement with the Community Drug and Alcohol Addiction team that I took the second and third parts of the Membership of the RCPsych Examinations. Preparation for these exams was long and intense. The stakes were high; if you didn't pass the exams you would not be allowed to progress from 'Core Training' into 'Higher Training'. But it felt like for me the stakes would be even higher. If for whatever reason you failed your exam, you were given the opportunity to repeat it. However, it always felt to me that if I did fail, it wouldn't be because the exams were tough (it wasn't uncommon that half of those taking the exam any given year would not pass it) or I was simply having an 'off day'. No. For me, according to the powers that be, if I failed the exam it would be because of my other interests and activities outside work.

I had delayed taking the second and third parts of the exam because I knew just how high the stakes were for me. I knew that if I failed the people further up the chain of command would come down on me like a ton of bricks. It was even mentioned in my exit report from my previous employer that there was a delay in taking the exams for these reasons, which wasn't true at all. I had arranged to take the third and final exam several months before the cut-off period. Moreover, the results had not yet been posted for the second part of the exams (i.e., 'Paper B') I had taken just after leaving the post and six months before I was due to transition to higher training. It was simple: a different set of rules applied to me. I could not fail the exams. I was determined to succeed in them partly because I didn't want to repeat the exam but also, I wanted to prove the naysayers wrong. So, I prepared intensively and my hard work paid off; the results of 'Paper B' were announced and I received one of the highest marks in the country. In other words, I smashed it! There was no better way to silence the detractors and haters.

The third and final part of the membership exams is called the 'Clinical Assessment of Skill and Applied Knowledge' (CASC). Unlike the first two exams, which were 'knowledge based', the CASC involved different stations whereby there would be a simulated patient and you were tasked with taking a focused history and examination from them. An examiner who was present throughout would ultimately decide if you passed or failed the station. The CASC was dreaded not because it was difficult (in fact, if anything, looking back this was the easiest of the three exams I had taken and was the one that I had the least time to prepare for). It was dreaded because of a phenomenon known as 'differential attainment'. This is a well-known phenomenon in postgraduate exams – not just psychiatry but other medical specialties – and a lot of effort and resources have gone into trying to resolve this issue. However, despite these attempts, differential attainment remains a problem in post-graduate medical exams.

For those not familiar with this phenomenon, as unfair as what you are about to read may be, I am not making this up. People of colour, on average, do worse in the CASC exam than their white counterparts even when all other variables are controlled for. This is irrespective of if you are an International Medical Graduate (i.e., you graduated from a medical school outside the United Kingdom) **or** if you graduated from a medical school in the United Kingdom and you are from a BAME background. In other words, your ethnicity and race are independent predictors of how you will fare in the CASC exam, with people of colour, on average, having statistically significant higher rates of failure no matter how much they prepared and how much they excelled in the other knowledge-based exams. It is impossible, as far as I am concerned, that racism does not play at least a partial role in 'differential attainment' and to say otherwise, in my opinion, is to ignore structural and systemic discrimination.

Through intensive preparation and by the grace of God, I passed the CASC exam with ease, obtained my Membership of the Royal College of Psychiatrists (MRCPsych) and was authorised to progress to the next stage of my training: 'Higher Training'. However, just before doing so I had to complete one more clinical placement, which was in the Bethlem Royal Hospital on the Anxiety Disorder Residential Unit (ADRU).

The Bethlem Royal is a world-renowned hospital the reputation (and notoriety) of which has seeped into public consciousness and popular culture. Bethlem is more commonly known as 'Bedlam' the connotations of which are unfortunately pejorative. Indeed, 'Bedlam' is a term that is often used synonymously with the asylums of the past during an era when 'mental illness' was referred to as 'lunacy' and stigmatising terms like 'lunatics' were used to denote people living with a mental health condition. Bedlam's infamous history has inspired multiple horror books and films over the years.

I always thought it was a shame that the Bethlem Royal was perceived in such a negative way even though a lot of this was due to how it was portrayed in fiction. The quality of the care that was provided in the hospital, from what I saw in my day-to-day work, was excellent. There were, however, incidents that occurred in Bethlem Royal that we learned about in our online mandatory training including the tragic death of Olaseni Lewis on 3 September 2010 after police subjected him to prolonged physical restraint. I will never forget watching the interviews with the Lewis' family members and loved ones in the Seni Lewis mandatory training, how devastated they all were and how much Olaseni was loved and respected by them and his local community. It was deeply affecting to see how dignified and graceful they were when talking about who Olaseni was as a person; that he was more than just a 'service user' (a term with negative connotations that is loathed by many persons receiving care), that he was a human being who cared deeply and passionately about people and who had given so much of himself to others through his kindness and selflessness. What was particularly moving was the family's determination to remember Olaseni and his contributions to improving the lives of others and to honour his legacy. But also, we must never, ever forget the way he died so that we can prevent such tragic deaths from ever happening again to other patients with mental health problems,

particularly patients of colour who are disproportionately affected by coercive practice.

The grounds for the Bethlem Royal Hospital itself are
beautiful. It is surrounded by 200 acres of green space
and the natural environment is conducive to mental
health recovery and resilience. The ADRU is a tertiary
service situated on the Bethlem Royal Hospital site. It
provides specialist assessment and care to patients living
with severe and debilitating anxiety disorders such as
obsessive-compulsive disorder. It remains one of the best
placements I have ever worked in. The team was absolutely incredible and the quality of care they provided
was outstanding. I have never met more compassionate
people and it doesn't surprise me that the outcomes for
patients following treatment in ADRU were so positive.

However, it wasn't just how they made patients feel, it's
how they made you as a member of the team feel too.
It was extraordinary. They immediately made me feel
like I was 'one of their own'. They had heard about my
accomplishments and activities but instead of being 'suspicious of my success' they were immensely proud of
me, which should have been the 'normal' reaction all
along. Once, a colleague of colour said something to me
I'll never forget: 'Ahmed, if only you were white, things
would have been so different for you. Your achievements
would have been celebrated even more and you would
be holding a senior leadership role.'

Unfortunately, my stay on ADRU was cut short. The
unit was forced to suspend services due to Covid-19,

which was spreading rapidly throughout the world. So, I was 'redeployed' to the Acute Adult Female Inpatient Ward in the Bethlem Royal Hospital. I don't think you can ever describe the scale of an event as colossal as the pandemic in a single chapter. That would not be fair and do justice to the people who were so adversely affected by it, both the patients and the people providing care to the patients (many, if not most of, whom would sooner or later become patients themselves due to working on the frontline and the inherent occupational hazards this entailed). The aim of the rest of this chapter is to share my personal and professional experiences and insights and reflections with you and to briefly describe how the pandemic affected patients, services, colleagues and me.

I was already a bit 'burnt out' after intense and prolonged preparation for the MRCPsych examinations. However, I was about to be exposed to a level of occupational stress I had never experienced, and I don't think anything could have prepared me for it. I, like many other health and social care professionals during the pandemic, was thrown into the deep end and we struggled to keep our heads above water. Tragically, it was not uncommon for health and social care professionals to 'drown'; studies have shown that suicidal behaviours amongst care providers increased during the pandemic and as a result of it. Where do we even begin to try to understand and explain the adverse effects it had on us and our patients?

There were so many pandemic-related political scandals. There was 'Partygate' in which the Prime Minister at the time, Boris Johnson, attended 'social gatherings' that breached the very Covid-19 laws that he and his cabinet conceived and implemented. Then there were the government contracts that were given out to private companies for the manufacturing and distribution of Personal Protective Equipment (PPE). The PPEs were so deficient, defective, faulty and poor in quality that they were deemed not fit for purpose and compromised the health, safety, welfare and lives of the healthcare professionals who donned them, and their patients. For such corporate greed and avarice to have infiltrated the ranks of politicians profoundly harmed the morale of the British public, especially the health and social care workers who were risking their lives. And this ultimately led to the downfall of Boris Johnson and arguably his political party.

On the ground, it felt like we were 'firefighting'; no matter how hard we worked to provide care to patients on our wards, stabilising them, and then discharging them back to the community, there was always a backlog of patients in emergency departments waiting for a hospital bed. But as the number of patients needing psychiatric admission dramatically increased, the number of staff available to care for them dramatically dropped. One by one, doctors, for example, would contract Covid-19 and would have to isolate for a fixed period. There was one point I remember I was the only doctor on the acute inpatient ward providing care to 20 severely unwell patients. Up to 50% of the medical workforce were forced to go on sick leave. Looking back, I don't know how we survived it. One colleague was so overwhelmed and burnt out, she literally hoped that she would contract Covid so that she could go on sick leave and be relieved of her duties. I completely understood why she felt this way. Colleagues of colour seemed to be especially vulnerable; there were increased rates of Covid-19 related deaths in doctors from BAME backgrounds and this data frightened us. Who would contract the virus next? Would it be me? Would I have to be put on a ventilator? What if there were not enough ventilators to go around, what then?

All these life-and-death scenarios constantly played out in our minds. Of course, it was damaging to our mental health. Although what was expected from us were superhuman things, we were very much human and as such we were vulnerable like everyone else. Moral injury, which is not uncommon in the care professions especially during times of crises, can occur after acting in a way or witnessing behaviours that go against one's values and morals: for example, not providing the level of care you are able to through no fault of your own but due to restraints imposed by limitations of equipment and the enormous demand for services. Such restraints and limitations contributed to 'spreading us out too thinly' and reduced the amount of time we could spend with each patient, thus inevitably affecting the quality of care we were able to provide. There were two patients among the many who stand out the most for me. The first patient, Mr A, was nearer the start of the life continuum, the second patient, Mr Z nearer the end.

Mr A, as the clinical notes usually go, 'is very well known to services'. He spent most of his teenage years as an inpatient on psychiatric wards. He had collected multiple psychiatric diagnoses over the years, and he had been trialled on numerous psychiatric medications, often a combination of antipsychotics and mood stabilisers. Like many people living with a mental health condition, the pandemic exacerbated his symptoms, and he was admitted involuntarily onto a mental health ward under Section 3 of the Mental Health Act – a treatment order that can last up to six months.

The patient's Responsible Clinician, the inpatient consultant psychiatrist, developed a rapport with him and a 'therapeutic alliance' whereby he was able to connect with the patient authentically, which contributed to the patient's gradual recovery and positive response to treatment. Mr A was making progress but wasn't quite clinically ready for discharge. He had sustained fractures to his upper limbs and for a long time had been on the waiting list for orthopaedic surgery.

One of the most striking things for me about Mr A was the relationship he had with his parents, especially his mother. I was deeply touched by how loving, caring and kind she was to him, even when he displayed 'challenging behaviours' that included physically assaulting her due to the nature and severity of his symptoms. However, his mother would always respond to her son with unconditional love. She was always there for him, and I found this very moving.

Unfortunately, there was a Covid-19 outbreak on the ward. The patient's mother was very concerned that her son might contract Covid-19 and that that would prevent him from having the operation they had been waiting so long for. She asked if he could have overnight leave with her whereby she would provide 24-hour care. That way, the risk of contracting Covid-19 would be reduced considerably, and it wouldn't compromise his chances of having the long-awaited surgery.

Mr A had made progress on the ward and plans were underway to transfer his care to his community team and discharge him. The patient had no history of self-harm or suicide attempts and was not currently suicidal. The reason for his admission was to treat the symptoms of his condition. Now that he had been responding positively to treatment, we felt it would be appropriate for him to stay with his family for a couple of days, have the operation, and return to the ward for a final assessment of his mental state prior to discharging him to the care of his community team. All people involved in Mr A's care, including and most importantly Mr A himself, agreed with the plan. Everything seemed to be going in the right direction.

However, soon after he went on leave from the ward, we received the tragic news from his family that the patient had died by suicide. The news shook the teams that were involved in his care; no one had expected or foreseen this, and some staff members were so traumatised they took leave to process and come to terms with the loss. No one, however, was affected as deeply as his mother.

Initially, she tried to maintain her composure whenever she visited the ward to meet with the inpatient consultant. However, I remember whilst she was sitting in the family room waiting for the consultant to arrive I asked her how she was feeling, and that is when the floodgates opened. I felt terrible for her. She had just experienced every mother's nightmare: outliving your child. I remember how initially she tried to hold back the tears, but she couldn't hold them back any longer, she was too wounded. We tried to comfort and console her as best as we could but to no avail; there was nothing more we could do at that moment other than be there for her.

Although Covid-19 didn't directly affect the tragic outcome, Mr A's untimely death was in the context of a pandemic. The pandemic certainly didn't help. It was the first patient suicide I faced in my career as a doctor. I thought about how cruel and devastating the symptoms of a mental health condition can be and how they have no regard for the lives of patients and their families. I thought about the specialist support that must be made available to families of loved ones who tragically die by suicide. I thought about government resources that are necessary to fund this specialist support that is so urgently needed. I thought about the suicide statistics that we are often taught about, but that behind each number is a patient – a human being – whose life was tragically cut short and the devastating effects this has on loved ones.

Mr Z, the older patient, was diagnosed with mental health problems later in life. Like many other patients with mental health problems, Mr Z also had coexistent physical health problems. This can be due to a variety of reasons but powerful psychiatric drugs like certain antipsychotics can be associated with weight gain and blood glucose dysregulation that, if left unmonitored and untreated, can cause major issues. Mr Z was frail and appeared emaciated. The symptoms of his mental health condition were so severe he lost all interest in living life and had profoundly reduced appetite and food and fluid intake. Indeed, I remember asking Mr Z once during a ward round if it felt more like he was existing rather than living and, after a brief delay and making eye contact with me, he replied yes. It wasn't so much what he said but how he said it that was so impactful. It seemed to me that he finally felt understood. For I had been there once myself, that dark and lonely place devoid of joy or happiness and full of dread, desolation and despair. Such questions are not taught in our training or found in psychiatric textbooks but rather are derived from our lived experiences of mental health conditions.

Mr Z, it seemed, had all but given up; however, he was not 'actively' suicidal, that is, he didn't have any plans or make any preparations to end his life, not that he had the volition or energy to do so. But when I asked him how he would feel if he went to sleep tonight and never woke up again, he replied that it wouldn't bother him at all but, in fact, it would be a welcome relief.

Despite our best efforts to contain the virus, it continued to spread relentlessly, and we declared a Covid-19 outbreak on the ward. The restrictions became even more stringent. Mr Z contracted Covid-19, however, because he was immunocompromised the virus wreaked havoc on his organs. His lungs began to fail, and he was struggling to breathe. I remember feeling so powerless and yes, even angry at this bug. It might sound ridiculous, but I felt like shouting at it and saying, 'Hey you, who do you think you are and what do you think you are doing? You are not welcome here! Stay out and leave our patients alone!' The symptoms of Mr Z's mental health condition were cruel enough. They robbed him of his will to live and sapped the energy required for basic breathing exercises. Covid-19 came along and was intent on stopping him from breathing altogether.

It felt like we were in a war zone; although our enemy was 'invisible' it was assaulting our patients, many of whom were unable to defend themselves because of the nature and degree of their mental health condition. Too many of our patients would tragically succumb to the wounds sustained from the battle against Covid-19 and die.

The paramedics arrived, connected Mr Z to a gas canister and initiated high-flow supplemental oxygen treatment. He was taken to the ambulance and was urgently conveyed to the emergency department in the general hospital for further treatment and support. That was the last time I ever saw Mr Z. We were informed that he tragically died. He didn't have any next-of-kin or family and even if he did, because of Covid-19 restrictions, they wouldn't have been able to remain by his side during his final breaths.

Looking back, I remember trying my best to stay positive for the sake of my patients but also for the sake of my sanity. I'd post selfies on social media of me donning a gown and with a smile on my face that was so big you could notice it even beneath my mask. BBC Radio London took notice and I contributed to a series about resilience and remaining positive during the pandemic. But as I've said time and time again, doctors are human too and we are vulnerable like everyone else. The pandemic also had a profound impact on us and the traumatic sequelae of our patients dying on our watch continues to haunt us to this day. I'm so sorry Mr A and Mr Z, I wish we could have done more to save you. Please forgive us.

12

Sorrow in the Holy Land

After passing my exams, somehow surviving the bru-tality of the pandemic, and completing my clinical placement in the Acute Female Adult Inpatient Ward at the Bethlem Royal Hospital, I transitioned to higher training and worked as a Specialist Registrar, which conferred certain privileges and benefits such as more autonomy and status. Moreover, whenever I was work-ing in emergency psychiatry I would be 'non-residential' meaning I wasn't based in the hospital (as had been the case when I was a 'core trainee'. I had served my time!). Instead I would be based at home and would only get called out to see the sickest patients who we felt needed to be admitted into hospital involuntarily. This was a game changer; the quality of my life improved consider-ably and so too did my financial situation.

The mental health benefits of financial security can-not be overstated. It is no exaggeration to say that as a 'core trainee' your financial situation is far from secure, even though you are a doctor. It was a hand-to-mouth existence that felt unfair given the years (and years!) of teaching and training we received, the skills and specialist knowledge we had to acquire and the rigorous exams we had to prepare for and pass.

It is for these reasons that junior doctors and more recently senior doctors throughout the United Kingdom have been striking to demand pay restoration (our pay has gone down in real terms if you take into consideration inflation over the years). The remuneration of a profession should reflect the responsibilities involved and what one had to go through to get to where they are. This topic has become heavily politicised, and doctors feel like they have been vilified and have been accused of being greedy. But, to emphasise again, doctors are human too and if we don't feel valued we will consider alternative options. Just like most people, we have others who are financially reliant upon us who we must support.

So, when a university based in Canada came knocking at my door asking me if I might be interested in working for them, I said I was. After a rigorous interview process, several trips to Canada and meeting with the faculty I took the plunge, signed the contract, and moved to Ontario in October 2023, where I am fortunate to be an Assistant Professor of Psychiatry. It wasn't an easy decision, and I left England and the NHS with a heavy heart. I already miss the patients, colleagues and my beloved Crystal Palace, which had been my home for the past three years. My plan is to take it 'one day at a time'. I will continue to conduct research on stigma reduction initiatives and global mental health. I will also continue to give talks and lectures to students and the public. I will also continue to provide care to patients with mental health problems. I want to seize this fantastic opportunity that I have been given and take full advantage of it so that I can continue to be of service to our communities and our world.

As I'm writing these words, I'm reclining on a seat in a cafe in Kiev, Ukraine, with what sounds like funky Ukrainian music playing in the background. You can be excused for wondering what on earth am I doing in the middle of a war zone? To be honest with you, aside from the sporadic sirens 'strongly encouraging' us to go to the designated shelter zone, it doesn't really feel like a war zone. In fact, I think I was the only person in the hotel to be 'strongly encouraged' to go to the shelter zone. Either it was a false alarm or people have become desensitised because they are not associated with air strikes and bombs. I appreciate that it wasn't always like this in the capital and that in other parts of Ukraine the situation is far worse.

Not so long ago, the WHO invited me to give a talk at the first mental health forum in Kiev, Ukraine, about the human rights of people living with mental health conditions. It's progressive to say the least that to 'qualify' I had to at least have lived experience of a mental health condition. It was an offer I couldn't refuse so I hopped onto the Polish Airline flight from Toronto to Warsaw and then took the 14-hour shuttle to Kiev. The session itself was incredibly powerful. After sharing my story with the audience about the traumatic effects that the 2006 Lebanon War had on me, one by one people stood up and started sharing their stories about how the Ukraine war was traumatising them and the adverse effects it was having on their mental health. You could feel the bonds in the auditorium between the audience members getting stronger and stronger and there was a real sense of solidarity like 'we are all in this together'. It was a life affirming experience.

I think about where I am today, by the grace of God, the adversity, barriers and obstacles I encountered and overcame and the wonderful people I've met along my journey who supported me. I remember that anxious 17-year-old boy on the plane from Beirut to London not having a clue what was waiting for him but believing with every fibre in his soul that one day he would realise his dream of becoming a doctor. I don't think I've done too badly since then!

Success certainly didn't come easily and on many occasions I was knocked down and thought about never getting up again. But somehow, no matter how devastating the blow was, I would get up, dust myself off and continue my perilous journey.

I am mindful of how extremely blessed I am to have had the opportunity to realise my dream. I thank God all the time for the opportunities I have been given and the many blessings that have been bestowed upon me.

Life isn't a level playing field and 'disadvantage is not distributed equally' with some of us having to work harder and longer than others to get the same chances in life through no fault of our own. It isn't fair and I understand why it hurts and why people are angry at the injustices (for anger is often the manifestation of pain).

The US sociologist Erving Goffman defines stigma as, 'A deeply discrediting attribute that reduces the bearer from a whole and usual person to a tainted and discounted one. The individual is thus disqualified from social acceptance.' That deeply discrediting attribute can be, but is certainly not limited to, a person's race, gender or faith. Not too long ago, women and girls were disadvantaged because of their gender (and continue to be disadvantaged in certain cultures and parts of the world and in many institutions and professions) and were denied access to medical schools (for example). People of colour were denied opportunities that their white counterparts were given for no reason other than the complexion of their skin. It should come as no surprise that there are certain employers who are more likely to invite applicants with European-sounding names compared to Muslim-sounding names, even if the two applicants have identical resumes.

For too many of us, the fight against stigma, racism and other types of discrimination rages on, often having detrimental effects on our mental health and wellbeing. You might have no control over your circumstances, but you can control how you react to them. So please don't give up. Keep on fighting that good fight. You've come too far and you've worked too hard to throw the towel in now.

Meanwhile, there is a terrible war being waged in Gaza with thousands of innocent and defenceless children and civilians being killed. On 16 October 2023, I posted on X:

I think it's wrong that many of us are afraid & intimidated to express our outrage when we witness crimes against humanity being carried out. Protesting peacefully is a human right.

I also posted on 20 October 2023:

If you know that being sensitised to a certain type of trauma can trigger a deterioration in your mental health, normalise not feeling guilty about distancing yourself from that trauma if at all possible. You don't ever want to return to that dark place if you can prevent it.

I haven't forgotten how being sensitised to the 2006 Lebanon War contributed to developing an episode of psychological distress. The symptoms were so devastating and the stigma so dehumanising that to this day, 17 years later, I am still processing the traumas and healing from the psychological wounds that were afflicted and sustained. I am being careful and cautious not to get too involved. It was a miracle I survived the first time. I am not convinced that I can endure another episode like the last one. That doesn't make me any less of a person or any 'less of a man'. I like to think I have become more resilient and mature, and I know what I have to do to protect my mental health and to prevent myself from becoming unwell again.

The killing of innocent Israeli civilians was deplorable, and I condemn this heinous and horrific attack in the strongest possible terms as I do the killing of innocent Palestinian civilians. To paraphrase Steinbeck, what the people of Palestine are going through is 'a sorrow that weeping cannot symbolise'. The Commissioner General of the United Nations Relief and Works Agency for Palestine Refugees in the Near East (UNRWA) Philippe Lazzarini stated on 15 October 2023 that:

> *There is not one drop of water, not one grain of wheat, not a litre of fuel that has been allowed to the Gaza Strip for the last eight days. In fact, an unprecedented human catastrophe is unfolding before our eyes . . .*

And:

> *[I]f we look at the issue of water, we all know water is life, and Gaza is running out of water and Gaza is running out of life . . .*

I think it is a violation of human rights that the accumulation of rain in cisterns in Gaza by the people of Palestine has been criminalised by the occupying force.

It is impossible to be detached from the tragic events unfolding in Gaza, especially since the violence has been spilling into Lebanon where my family lives and the situation in the region remains volatile.

Anti-Semitic and Islamophobic attacks have also been on the rise. Dr Omar Suleiman, an Imam based in Dallas, Texas, and Professor at Southern Methodist University posted a comment on his social media platform decrying the brutal killing of Wadea Al-Fayoume, a 6-year-old Palestinian-American boy who was stabbed to death in Chicago because, according to the perpetrator of this barbaric act, he wanted to 'eliminate a Palestinian before they grow up.' The perpetrator reportedly developed these violent views after watching the news about the war in Gaza. The tragic death is a painful reminder that Islamophobia can be lethal. It is also an important reminder that politics and the media play major roles in contributing to the rise and spread of Islamophobia.

So, where does that leave us and, more specifically, people living with mental health conditions? The world is certainly not in the best of shape at the moment. I mentioned earlier that you can protect your mental health if you 'distance' yourself from certain traumas that you know will trigger you. It might be helpful if you disable notifications and limit the amount of screen time even if only temporarily. However, I understand that many of us cannot 'turn a blind eye and a deaf ear' to all the suffering, especially if it concerns a community you feel you belong to. I think having a balanced and measured approach would be sensible: the moment you feel you are approaching your threshold, disengage immediately. On 25 October 2023, I posted on X a personal quote:

Normalise doing whatever it takes to protect your peace and your mental health, they are just too precious.

The atrocities in the Holy Land have reminded me that there are so many things that we can't take for granted. Populating a gratitude diary, even posting content on social media expressing what you are grateful for, can be associated with positive health outcomes. I posted the following content on my platforms both of which must have resonated with my online community, given the thousands of likes I received for them:

I returned to my hotel room & I switched on the light & it was working. I turned the tap on & water flowed out of it. We can never, ever take these things for granted.

And:

I woke up this morning in the comfort of my own home. I had a roof over my head & it was warm & cozy. I didn't think about the security of my accommodation, if a bomb would be dropped at any moment destroying everything. War is so terrible. I pray for all the civilians affected.

My thoughts now turn to people living with severe mental illness. Are we doing enough for people suffering from these conditions? Certainly not. It is worth emphasising that a government will be judged by how the most vulnerable amongst us, that is, those living with severe mental illness, are treated. In this regard, governments have failed spectacularly. It's not only the lack of specialist care, but also the quality of that care that are major issues.

We need to pioneer innovative approaches in the treatment of severe mental illness. Such an approach must be holistic and grounded on a 'biopsychosocial' model as opposed to a 'biobiobio' model that almost exclusively gives primacy to psychotropic medications and excludes psychosocial interventions. Mental health care must also be based on a human rights framework, and it is heartening that the WHO's QualityRights initiative, which embraces a human rights model in mental health, is gaining global traction and is starting to be implemented in countries throughout the world.

I certainly don't have all the answers but that was never the intended purpose of this book. Maybe you are a student and you experienced trauma that derailed you. You were forced to interrupt university and when you needed care and compassion the most, you received ridicule and rejection instead. You eventually sought support and you slowly started to notice some improvements in your mental health, and you resumed your studies. But recovery is a slippery slope at the best of times, and there are occasions when it can feel that you are taking one step forward and two steps back. The important thing is not to give up and to keep giving it your best shot. That's the most we can do.

If you did have to take time out, when you do resume your studies you are no longer with the same cohort you started with. You either try hard to integrate with the new cohort but are socially excluded (due to stigma and/ or the establishment of cliques); or you just don't have it in you and/or you're not in the mood to start all over again. You can feel isolated, and the social disconnectedness is getting to you. Maybe you'll chance upon this book in the university or local library as I once chanced upon a memoir from a Scottish man about living with a mental health condition characterised by 'oscillations in emotion'. I was able to relate to his mental health struggles and such identification can make you feel less alone and can be comforting. There is 'solace in shared experience' after all. If this book has planted the seeds of hope into your heart, mind, body and soul then it has served its purpose.

I am honoured and privileged that you joined me on this journey, and I can't thank you enough for coming this far. Please never forget that you are precious, and that the world is a better place with you in it. I know it's difficult to internalise those words cognitively and emotionally, to both know them and feel them. But the words are true.

Please don't make a decision that has permanent consequences based on a temporary situation or feeling. I know it might not seem like it, but the feeling is transient, and it will pass. Choose life. Try to 'ride it out' and don't do it alone. Go to your local community centre, mosque, synagogue, church or temple and see a trained health professional like your GP or psychiatrist. If you are feeling suicidal and you are concerned you'll act upon these thoughts, go to your local hospital (a mental health emergency is no less an emergency than a physical health emergency and both need the highest level of care and compassion). Help is out there, it can be difficult to find I know, but it's there and there is no shame in seeking it.

I do not want to misinform you; not everyone recovers and as I mentioned earlier, we are not doing enough for people living with severe mental illness. This is scandalous at best and a human rights violation at worst. Our hearts go out to you.

However, recovery is a reality for the many, and not for the few, this much is true. I hope my story outlined in this book is further evidence to prove that not only can we survive but, dare I say it, we can thrive too.

I was once a slouch on a couch, and I was so out of shape that my GP was going to start me on medication to lower my cholesterol. I didn't even have the energy to get out of bed, let alone go for a run. That's why tidying your bed can feel like such a monumental achievement and it is for those amongst us battling the debilitating symptoms of major depressive disorder, so give yourself a pat on the back. My sedentary lifestyle whilst I was in the throes of a mental health condition increased my risk of developing life-threatening conditions such as ischaemic heart disease and stroke, thus rendering me vulnerable to premature death. I am proud that I run 15 km daily. Celebrate your victories and if you want to, share them with your online community.

I know it can be a hell of a lot easier said than done, but ignore the haters, naysayers and gaslighters, especially the keyboard warriors and trolls who are hellbent on focusing on your faults and ignoring all the positive contributions you make online and beyond. Often, it is more a reflection on them than it is on you. I came across a quote once that is pertinent but unfortunately I cannot find the source of it, 'Many people are wounded children trapped in adult bodies.' A lot of these critics may have unresolved issues that they are not conscious of so try not to take what they post about you personally. That doesn't excuse them in any way, shape or form. On the contrary, as I've stated before, accountability can deter perpetrators from committing further online attacks in the future. But, for the sake of salvaging your own sanity, 'continue scrolling'.

After you finish reading this book and you go forth into this world, remember we each carry wounds of varying depths and it is the wounds that can't be seen that are indeed the deepest. Our wounds are nothing to be ashamed about. My wounds are my badges of honour and to paraphrase the Persian mystic Rumi himself, 'Our wounds are where the Light enters you'.

I'll close by saying:

We each are fighting battles others have absolutely no idea about. So in a world where we can be anything, be kind. We must also extend that kindness to ourselves.

Protect your hearts and protect your minds.
Never stop believing in yourself.
And never stop dreaming.
Dr Ahmed Hankir, *Breakthrough*. Kiev, Ukraine October
  2023

Acknowledgements

I must firstly and above all else thank Allah for the many blessings that He has bestowed upon me. I believe it's a miracle that I survived and that I was able to come this far in life. I would never have been able to do so without His mercy and compassion. With guidance from His words inscribed eternally in His Book and from the teachings of His prophet Mohammed PBUH I was able to overcome trauma, recover and realise my dreams of becoming a doctor and a psychiatrist.

I want to thank my mum Mariam Hankir for her unconditional love. It was Mum who taught me from a young age the importance of being kind, gentle and respectful towards others. Like other mothers of persons living with a mental health condition, she was heartbroken and devastated to discover what had happened to me. However, she never lost faith in me, and always believed that I would triumph in the face of adversity and succeed.

I want to thank my father Dr Zakaria Hankir 'hakeem shaab' or 'the people's doctor' who was and remains my role model and who inspired me to become a doctor. Dad instilled in me the values of honesty, integrity and courage but also a 'never-give-up' attitude. It was dad who taught me the importance of working hard and helping others who are less fortunate than ourselves. Dr Zakaria Hankir continues to selflessly serve the most vulnerable people in our world.

I must thank my brother Khodor Hankir or 'Big Bro' who endured much suffering and struggling to make life easier for me. I have lost count how many times Khodor bailed me out of trouble when I was in medical school. I am always able to count and rely on Khodor and I can't thank him enough for everything that he has done for me.

I thank my twin brother Dr Mohammed Hankir – one of the leading neuroscientists and experimentalists in the cellular and molecular mechanisms of weight loss in the world – whose companionship throughout my journey helped to make me feel less alone. 'Bro Mo' always made me feel that I could realise my dreams and he would always encourage me to be ambitious and to aim high. Dr Mohammed Hankir is a scientist of uncompromising principle, and he inspired me to work harder through his own discipline and work ethic. His love and passion for science, culture and the arts is truly unique.

I thank my younger brother Osman Hankir or 'Bro Oz' for his humour and his intellect which helped me to cope with my difficulties. Bro Oz is perhaps the most introverted out of all 'the boys' but also perhaps the most intuitive and thoughtful in his concern for me when I was unwell.

Acknowledgements

I thank my sisters Yasmine and Zahra for their unending affection and love. I remember how upset they were when they saw me at my worst. It was an important reminder of how much I meant to them and how deeply they cared for me. The happiness they experience whenever I achieve a goal in my life is especially heartening.

I thank my best friend Wassim whom I have mentioned often in this book for his loyalty and for his unwavering support throughout the years.

I thank the Salmon family who supported me during the 2006 Lebanon War when I was a medical student in Manchester. The Salmon family welcomed me into their home in London and cared for me as if I was one of their own. I would never have qualified as a doctor without their help.

I thank Prof. Ged Byrne who was the Dean of the Teaching Hospital I was allocated to when I was a medical student. Prof. Byrne saw me when I was at my worst during the 2006 Lebanon War. I have no doubt that if it was anyone else who was Dean at the time, I would have been kicked out of medical school. But he understood that what I needed was treatment, not punishment. Prof. Byrne's depth and breadth of heart and mind were crucial factors that contributed to my convalescence. I would never have qualified as a doctor without his humanity, humility and kindness.

I thank Dr Rashid Zaman who was my mentor when I was a medical student in Manchester. I met Dr Zaman at the 2009 Biennial International Conference on Mental Health at Cambridge University of which he is the Director. This was when I was still in recovery. Since we met, Rashid has been there for me every step of the way, through the good times and the bad. He saw in me that which I could not see in myself. He taught me how to be a good doctor, psychiatrist, researcher and teacher. Without Dr Zaman I would never have achieved my career goals. Dr Zaman's calming presence in my life brought much needed comfort and relief during periods of distress. Rashid is a dear friend of mine who never gave up on me and who would always support me whenever I needed it.

I want to thank Prof. Ted Carrick for his endless energy, exuberance and effervescence and for his unwavering support over the past 10 years. I met Prof. Carrick when he was teaching me at a class in Harvard and we made an instant connection. Prof. Carrick was very much like a father figure and despite the distance between us (he lives in Cocoa Beach in Florida) I always felt he was close to me. Prof. Carrick was a lifeline on many occasions in my personal life but he also played an instrumental role in propelling my career forward in North America.

I thank Dr Rajesh Mohan and Dr Brendon Stubbs who were my closest friends in London, UK. Raj and Brendon would often reach out to me to make sure that I was okay and, if I wasn't, they would immediately meet up with me and support me until I was. The meals we would have together have always been joyous and uplifting occasions. I can only describe the friendship we have as a thing of beauty. It's so powerful that whenever we see each other we always have our arms wrapped around each other or we would always be embracing each other. Such open displays of affection between men are not common, however, they should be given how they can help to cheer you up and make you feel valued.

I thank Dr Eduardo Iacoponi who was my Educational Supervisor when I was specialising in academic psychiatry in London, UK. Dr Iacoponi always had my back especially when colleagues at work were giving me a tough time. He would always bring out the best in me and I can't thank him enough for empowering me to realise my potential. Dr Iacoponi always made time for me. He would always listen to me and be gentle, kind and respectful to me. He never spoke down to me but instead always elevated me. Dr Iacoponi is inspirational in the true sense of the word, and I can only hope that I have the same lasting impact on my juniors that he has on me.

I thank Prof. Fiona Gaughran who was my Clinical Supervisor when I was training in London, UK. Fiona was an endless source of kindness and compassion and is the best clinical supervisor I've ever had in my entire life. Apart from benefiting from her vast knowledge and expertise, the weekly supervision sessions I had with Prof. Gaughran were, no exaggeration, life affirming. There is no other consultant psychiatrist who has touched my mind and heart the way Fiona has.

I thank Dr Jon Goldin, a Consultant in Child and Adolescent Psychiatry in London, UK for his friendship.

Jon's kindness, compassion and humility made it easy for me to reach out to him whenever I experienced hardship. Dr Goldin cares deeply about persons living with mental health conditions, especially younger people and he inspired me to be the best psychiatrist that I can be.

I thank Dr Michelle Funk at the WHO for her friendship, kindness and compassion and for her unwavering support in my personal and professional lives. Michelle always made time for me despite her hectic schedule, and she always made herself emotionally available for me too. Dr Funk was the person who, through her own relentless, pioneering and selfless work, inspired me to promote the human rights of persons living with mental health conditions and psychosocial disabilities. It was Dr Funk who provided me with the platform that amplified my voice so that it would echo in the chambers of the WHO.

I thank Prof. Steve Moffic in Milwaukee whom I consider to be my 'spiritual father'. I have been fortunate to co-edit several textbooks with Steve on religion and psychiatry. Throughout this period, we became very close. I think Steve's most striking qualities are his patience, gentleness, erudition, curiosity and his incredible work ethic. I have also had the good fortune to meet Steve's wife Rusti with whom I am also very close. Steve and Rusti bring light and colour to this world.

I thank Dr Tedros, the Director General of the WHO for restoring my faith in humanity and for reminding me why I decided to become a doctor in the first place:

to selflessly serve society, to help and to heal persons afflicted with physical and/or mental health conditions and to improve the quality of their lives as best as we can. It is no exaggeration to state that Dr Tedros makes this world a better place to live in.

I thank Annie Knight at Wiley for approaching me and for suggesting that I write this book. These words were always inside my mind and heart but Annie helped to bring them out onto these pages.

I thank Alice Hadaway and Stacey Rivera at Wiley for their assistance throughout the process of writing this book.

I thank Sunnye Collins, my Development Editor, for painstakingly going through the manuscript and editing it and combing out all the tangles.

I thank my X/Twitter community for all the 'likes' and love they have given me and the kind and caring comments they posted in relation to my content and activities. It really is amazing the amount of positivity and goodwill I receive from my X/Twitter community who have kept me company over the past five years as I navigated the precarious waters of psychiatric training.

Most importantly, I thank the patients to whom I have been fortunate to care for. Thank you for sharing your stories with me, for trusting me with your lives, and for contributing to my professional growth and personal development. I remain humbled by your dignity, fortitude and grace. You are the ultimate teachers and I have learned invaluable lessons from each and every one of you. Thank you for continuously inspiring me to be a better doctor and to be the best version of myself that I can be.

Index

Index

Index

Index

Index